Almost Paradise

Books by Sam Hamill

POETRY

Petroglyphs

The Calling Across Forever

The Book of Elegiac Geography

Triada

Animae

Fatal Pleasure

The Nootka Rose

Passport

A Dragon in the Clouds

Mandala

Destination Zero: Poems 1970–1995

Gratitude

Dumb Luck

Almost Paradise: New and Selected Poems and Translations

ESSAYS

At Home in the World

Bashō's Ghost

A Poet's Work: The Other Side of Poetry

POETRY IN TRANSLATION

Night Traveling

The Lotus Lovers

The Same Sea in Us All: Poems of Jaan Kaplinski

The Art of Writing

Catullus Redivivus

The Art of Writing: Lu Chi's Wen Fu

Banished Immortal: Poems of Li Po

The Wandering Border: Poems of Jaan Kaplinski

Facing the Snow: Poems of Tu Fu

Narrow Road to the Interior and Other Writings of Bashō

Only Companion: Poems from Japanese

The Infinite Moment: Poems from Ancient Greek

Endless River: Li Po and Tu Fu

Midnight Flute: Poems from Chinese

The Sound of Water: Haiku by Bashō, Buson and Issa

River of Stars: Selected Poems of Yosano Akiko

The Spring of My Life and Selected Haiku of Issa

The Essential Chuang Tzu

Crossing the Yellow River: Three Hundred Poems from the Chinese

The Poetry of Zen

Tao Te Ching

Almost Paradise

NEW AND SELECTED POEMS
AND TRANSLATIONS

∞

Sam Hamill

SHAMBHALA
Boston & London ■ 2005

Shambhala Publications, Inc.
Horticultural Hall
300 Massachusetts Avenue
Boston, MA 02115
www.shambhala.com

9 8 7 6 5 4 3 2 1
First Edition
Printed in the United States of America

⊛ This edition is printed on acid-free paper that meets the American
National Standards Institute z39.48 Standard. Distributed in the United
States by Random House, Inc., and in Canada by Random House of
Canada Ltd

Interior design and composition: Greta D. Sibley & Associates

Library of Congress Cataloging-in-Publication Data
Hamill, Sam.
Almost paradise: new and selected poems and translations/Sam
Hamill.
p. cm.
English translations of poems in Greek, Latin, Chinese, Japanese,
Estonian, and poems by Sam Hamill.
Includes bibliographical references.
ISBN 1-59030-184-6 (acid-free paper)
1. Poetry—Translations into English. I. Title.
PS3558.A4235A79 2005
811'.54—DC22
2004016049

To Gray Foster and Eron Hamill

"I know what I have given you.
I do not know what you have received."
—*Antonio Porchia*
(translated by W. S. Merwin)

Growing Strong

He who wishes to strengthen his spirit
must adandon reverence and submission.
He will honor some laws,
but mostly he will break both law and custom
and he will stray from the accepted, inadequate straight path.
He will be taught much by many sensual pleasures.
He will not fear the destructive act;
half the house must be torn down.
This way he will grow virtuous toward knowledge.

—C. P. Cavafy (*translated by Aliki Barnstone*)

Our lives begin to end the day we become silent about
things that matter.

—*Martin Luther King, Jr.*

Contents

Acknowledgments   xiii

Traveling Companions
SELECTED TRANSLATIONS   1

Ancient Greek Poets   3
    Sappho   3
    Anakreon   5
    Asklepiados   8
Catullus   10
Chinese Poets   13
    Lao Tzu   13
    Chuang Tzu   18
    Lu Chi   21
    Wang Wei   26
    Li Po   29
    Tu Fu   32
    Yuan Chen   36
    Su Tung-p'o   39
    Li Ch'ing-chao   41
Japanese Poets   44
    Saigyō   44
    Ikkyū   47
    Bashō   49
    Buson   56
    Ryōkan   58
    Issa   61
    Yosano Akiko   71
Jaan Kaplinski   74

Almost Paradise
NEW AND SELECTED POEMS   79

The Nets   81

A Lover's Quarrel   81

Gnostology   85

A Cold Fire   87

To Kevin, Who Mourns   88

To John Logan from La Push   88

Natural History   89

Kah Tai Purgatorio   91

Requiem   92

George Seferis in Sonora   104

Hellenic Triptych   107

A Word for Spring   109

Reading Seferis   110

Old Bones   113

Black Marsh Eclogue   114

A Dragon in the Clouds   115

The Gift of Tongues   116

"True Illumination Is Habitude"   117

Historical Romance   119

Seated Figure   127

Dresden Cattle   127

Blue Monody   128

Getting It Wrong Again   146

Scrutability   147

Lifer   148

Two Pines   148

Mountains and Rivers without End   149

Ten Thousand Sutras   149

Kannon   151

Destination Zero   151

What the Water Knows   165

Three Stitches   166

To Gary Snyder   166

To Adrienne Rich   170

After Coltrane's "I'll Get By"   173

Seattle Spring   173

"One Who Studies the Past . . . "   174

To Hayden Carruth   174

Sisyphus   182

To Hayden Carruth on His Eightieth Birthday   185

To Bill and Kris   186

Song and Dance   189

Weasel, Crow, and Coyote on the Dharma Trail   191

Why Crows are Noisy   192

Rising   192

Lost in Translation   194

To W. S. Merwin   195

In Memoriam, Morris Graves   197

For Kyra Gray O'Daly   199

All Here   199

Midsummer   199

Seducing the Sparrow   201

New Math   202

The Orchid Flower   203

Organic Form   204

Little Epic Elegy   204

Not Meaning, but Being   205

A Woodsplitter's Meditation   206

To Amy, before Her Wedding   208

Reply to T'ao Ch'ien   210

The Goldfinch   210

Strawberry Picking   211

To Yoshinaga Sayuri   211

The New York Poem   213

State of the Union, 2003   215

Poem in the Margins of the Shōyō Roku   216

Elegy   216

Nothing Quite So Cold   217

Sheepherder Coffee   218

Summer Rain   218

On Being Asked about Retirement   220

"Praise a Fool and Make Him Useful"   221

A Pisan Canto   222

After a Winter of Grieving   255

Notes on Traveling Companions   257

Acknowledgments

Thanks to:

BOA Editions, Ltd. for permission to reprint poems from *Dumb Luck* (2002) and *Gratitude* (1998), and from *Crossing the Yellow River: Three Hundred Poems from the Chinese* (2000).

New Directions for permission to reprint poems from *The Infinite Moment: Poems from Ancient Greek* (1991). Special thanks to the late James Laughlin.

Milkweed Editions for permission to reprint a portion of *The Art of Writing: Lu Chi's Wen Fu* (2000).

Tricia Treacy at Pointed Press for beautiful limited editions of *Saigyo* and *A Pisan Canto*.

Harry and Sandra Reese at Turkey Press for the beautiful limited edition, *Night Traveling*, my first translations from Chinese.

Other selections originally appeared in the following: *A Pisan Canto* [Part One] was first published by thedrunkenboat.com (thanks to Rebecca Seiferle), and as a chapbook by Floating Bridge Press, 2004; *Catullus Redivivus* (Blue Begonia Press, 1968); *Destination Zero: Poems 1970–1995* (White Pine Press, 1995); *The Same Sea in Us All* (Breitenbush Books, 1986); *The Wandering Border* (Copper Canyon Press, 1987); and from Shambhala Publications: *Tao Te Ching* (2005), *Narrow Road to the Interior & Other Writings of Basho* (2000); *The Essential Chuang Tzu* (1998); *Midnight Flute* (1994); *Only Companion* (1997); *River of Stars: Selected Poems of Yosano Akiko* (1997); *Spring of My Life & Selected Haiku of Kobayashi Issa* (1997); *The Sound of Water* (2000); *The Erotic Spirit* (1995); *The Poetry of Zen* (2004).

Special thanks to: William Anthony O'Daly—through it all; Peter Turner, editor, friend and nurturer through two decades; the late Denise Levertov, who helped shape many of these poems while complaining that I spent too much time translating—loyal friend and teacher; Hayden Carruth, elder brother; brother Yusuke Keida—my undying gratitude.

Traveling Companions

SELECTED TRANSLATIONS

❧ Ancient Greek Poets

SAPPHO
(CA. 630 B.C.E.)

He is almost a god, a man beside you,
enthralled by your talk, by your laughter.
Watching makes my heart beat fast
because, seeing little, I imagine much.
You put a fire in my cheeks.
Speech won't come. My ears ring.
Blind to all others, I sweat and I stammer.
I am a trembling thing, like grass,
an inch from dying.

So poor I've nothing to lose, I must gamble . . .

∞

If you lusted after something noble or decent,
had you not filled your talk with the vile—

had you told the truth, shame would not
force you to turn away your eyes.

∞

Eros seizes and shakes my very soul
like the wind on the mountain
shaking ancient oaks.

The Pleiades disappears,
the pale moon goes down.

After midnight, time blurs:
sleepless, I lie alone.

Someday you will be dead.
Even our memory of you will die.

You think you've earned a wreath
of laurels to crown your pretty head?

Unknown even as you wander
the infinities of Hell, you belong

among the shadows of the dead.

High on the upper, outermost bough,
the sweet apple blushes.

Below, the party-goers saw, thirsted,
but could not touch it.

Muse of the Golden Throne,
raise your voice again to sing
that song learned from the Sage of Teos,

that song of ample land and fair women,
his sweet singing
made palpable, a gift for us.

ANAKREON
(CA. 570 B.C.E.)

If Profit offered immortality for gold,
hoarding might be understandable—
a few gold coins for Thanatos,
and he'd pass on in the night.

But since a life is not for sale,
it's senseless to waste the tears.
Death, like life, is our fate.
Gold is only another emptiness.

Come, pour sweet wine for me
so we can drink, friends.
Or I might find a feather bed
and honor Aphrodite's rites.

Who cares about the filthy rich
excesses of the Boss of Sardis?

He's nothing to me. I won't
be bothered with tyrants.

I'm concerned with covering my head
with a garland of roses;

I'm concerned only with the moment,
tomorrow has other revisions and disclosures.

Now, under this cloudless sky,
cast your dice, pour wine for Dionysus—

soon enough a day will come
bringing consumption or diseases.

Weaving a garland long ago,
somehow I found Eros
there among the roses.

I clutched him by his wings
and thrust him into wine
and drank him quickly.

And ever since, deep inside,
I feel the wings of Eros
gently tickling.

Eros, playing among the roses,
didn't see the bee.
Stung, he howled,
he screamed to Aphrodite,

"I'm dying! Mother! I'm dying!
I was bitten by
a snake with wings!"
And she kissed him and replied,

"It will pass. It was only a bee,
my darling, but think
how long the suffering
of all those who feel your sting."

Count, if you can, every leaf on every tree.
And count each wave that comes ashore from every possible sea—
then you might number my plethora of lovers.

Compute if you can the countless loves of Athens,
the infinite passions of Korinth,
and Achaea where the women take your breath away.

Write down the names of all my loves in Lesbos,
remember their names from Ionia, from Karios and Rhodos,
their names from passionate dark Syria,

and from Krete where Eros runs wild in the streets.
How can I number my many loves in India, in Baktria?
How many did I love in Cadiz?

ASKLEPIADOS

(CA. 320 B.C.E.)

Didyme waved an olive branch at me,
and now my heart melts like wax
embraced by flame.

Oh, I know, I know. She is dark.
And so's the coal before the spark
that makes it burn like roses.

∞

It is eternally winter,
these endless nights I pace
before your door, rain-
soaked, tormented
by desires fueled
by your lies, Deceiver!

It was not the kiss
of Kypris
brought me low,
but an arrow
in the heart,
hot as fire.

∞

Think how unspeakably sweet
the taste of snow at mid-summer,
how sweet a kind spring breeze
after the gales of winter.

But as we all discover,
nothing's quite as sweet

as one large cloak
wrapped around two lovers.

Nico's bedroom talents entice men
to cross the farthest seas,
she brings stripling boys
their wildest fantasies.

And then she dangles at their breast
a single translucent amethyst,
a gift from Kypris,
and a parting kiss.

Once I lay down with Hermione
who wore a gold-stitched gown
fit for any queen.

And the song sewn round:
"Love me now and love me more
when I, with another, lay down."

✄ *Catullus*
(CA. 60 B.C.E.)

If I didn't love you more than even my eyes,
my charming Calvus, for your gift
you'd've earned a wrath as odious as Vatinius'—
whatever have I said or done
to urge these poets on?
To hell with your uppity clientele.
Bastard lot of wretched hacks!
But if, as I suspect, this noble gift
comes your way from Sulla, the professor,
it's quite another matter, and I'll be content:
that way, your efforts won't be for nothing.
My god, what a ghastly book this is
you send your old friend, Catullus.
It was death for this year's Saturnalia,
a day that should have been my best.
You'll pay for this.
By dawn, I'll be at the bookstalls
collecting the venom of Aquinas and his ilk
to return your gift in kind.
You and your anthology poets
can go home on your metric feet—
you were but one small pestilence
in an age of grief and disease.

∞

He is like a god,
he is greater than a god
sitting beside you listening

to your laughter. You make me crazy.
Seeing you, my Lesbia, takes my breath away.
My tongue freezes, my body
is filled with flames,
bells ring, and night invades my eyes.
You exult in it, the very thing
that brought down noble houses and great cities.

My woman says she'd rather have me
than anyone. Even if Jupiter proposed,
she says. But what an eager woman says to lovers
should be written out in winds and waters.

Surely, you'll come dine with me, my Fabullus,
and soon, if your luck holds out
and provided you supply the liquor
and the food, and bring a lovely girl,
and of course your usual witty conversation,
and your belly-laughs. Bring these, friend,
and you'll eat well, for I, Catullus,
have a purse full of cobwebs.
I offer you only a taste of love
and the elegance of metaphysics;
I'll offer you perfumes
my woman swiped from Cupid and Venus—
When you smell that, my Fabullus, you'll ask
the gods to make you nothing but a nose.

The Annals of Volusius, those shitty sheets,
should fulfill my sweetheart's promise:
she promised Cupid and Venus

that if I should once again return
and halt my barbed iambics,
she would choose the best
of the worst poet to burn for the gods
with some unfortunate tree.
Now goddess of the blue sea,
you who inhabit
the Adriatic tavernas,
count this task completed
if this will meet the vow:
the witless, cracker-barrel rustic
Annals of Volusius, those truly shitty sheets.

Give up all thought of gratitude,
don't ever expect a 'thank you' in return.
All this earns ingratitude, benevolence earns nothing.
It is tiresome. Nothing's so oppressive
as the man who called me friend.

✻ Chinese Poets

Lao Tzu
(CA. 500 B.C.E.)

FROM Tao Te Ching

Tao defined is not the constant Tao.
No name names its eternal name.

The unnamable is the origin of heaven and earth;
named, it is the mother of the ten thousand things.

Emptied of desire, we see the mystery;
filled with desire, we see the manifestation of things.

Two names emerge from a single origin,
and both are called mysterious,

and the mystery itself is the gateway to perception. [1]

Beauty and ugliness have one origin.
Name beauty, and ugliness is.
Recognizing virtue recognizes evil.

Is and *is not* produce one another.
The difficult is born in the easy,
long is defined by short, the high by the low.

Instrument and voice achieve one harmony.
Before and *after* have places.
That is why the sage can act without effort
and teach without words,
nurture things without possessing them,
and accomplish things without expecting merit:

only one who makes no attempt to possess it
cannot lose it. [2]

Heaven is eternal. The earth endures.

The reason for heaven's eternity and earth's endurance
is that they do not live for themselves only,
and therefore may live forever.

The sage steps back but remains in front,
the outsider always within.

Self is realized through selflessness. [7]

It's best to be like water,
nurturing the ten thousand things
without competing,
flowing into places people scorn,
very like the Tao.
Make the earth a dwelling place.
Cultivate heart and mind.
Practice diffidence.
Stand by your word.
Govern with equity.
Serve skillfully.
Act in a timely way,

without contentiousness,
free of blame. [8]

Looking and not seeing it,
we call it invisible;
listening and not hearing it,
we call it inaudible;
reaching and not touching it,
we call it ethereal.

These three aspects of it cannot be grasped,
but contribute to the one.
Its rising brings no dawn,
its setting brings no darkness;
it goes on and on, unnamable,
returning into nothingness.

Its form is formless.
Its image is invisible.
Meeting it, you cannot see its face.
Following it, you cannot see its back.

Hold to the ancient Tao
to grasp the here-and-now.
Discovering how things have always been
brings one into harmony with the Way. [14]

Skillful travelers leave no tracks.
Skillful speech leaves no doubt.
Good accounting needs no abacus.

Good doors may neither bolt nor bar,
and yet remain secure.

A good knot needs neither rope nor thread,
and yet cannot be opened.

Thus the sage always rescues people
for a reason, rejecting none,
extending compassion to all life,
rejecting none.

This is enlightened practice.

Therefore the one who lacks no goodness
is fit to lead those who lack,
and those who lack
are themselves a resource.

"Esteem for no master,
no love for the student,"
perplexes even the wise.

Call this the essential mystery. [27]

Of all things,
arms are least auspicious,
despised by people.
The sage spurns arms.

At home, inhabit the feminine.
At war, the masculine needs weapons.

Arms serve evil.
They are the tools of those who oppose wise rule.
Use them only as a last resort.

Calm restraint serves best.
Don't be seduced by glory.

Those who find glory in arms
rejoice in the slaughter of people.
Those who rejoice in slaughter
never attain their true place in the world.

On auspicious occasions, honor the left;
when mourning, honor the right.
Second in command stands on the left,
and the commander on the right,
speaking as if at a funeral.
With the slaughter of multitudes,
we have grief and sorrow.

Every victory is a funeral. [31]

Chuang Tzu
(369–286 B.C.E.)

Yao tried to pass the rulership of All-under-heaven to Hsu Yu, saying, "The sun and moon are out, and yet the torches remain burning. Doesn't too much light just make things all the more difficult? If we irrigate during the rainy season, aren't we exercising poor management? If you would only stand and assume your rightful place, All-under-heaven would be well governed. Although I try to model my conduct on yours, I can be no more than the 'personator' at the sacrifices whose duty it is to represent the spirits of departed ancestors. I see what a mess I've made of things! Please accept rulership."

Hsu Yu replied, "You're ruling All-under-heaven, so it's being ruled. If I assumed power, what would I be taking but a title? Aren't titles and names merely the servants, the familiar guests of the real? And why would I want to become a servant of myself? The little sparrow nesting in the forest needs only a single branch; the mole drinking from the river drinks but one bellyful. Go home, my lord, and sit under a shady tree. I have no use at all for All-under-heaven. When the cook fails to govern his kitchen, the high priest and the 'personator' don't leap over wine casks in a rush to 'succeed' him."

Chieh Wu said to Lien Shu, "I listened to the Madman of Ch'u, Chieh Yu. Big talk. But there was no thusness in it. It went out and on and on, but it never came back to anything. I was shocked and frightened by it. He went on and on like the River of Heaven (Milky Way), flowing without end. It was just too much. And all without the warmth of human feeling."

Lien Shu asked, "What did he say?"

"He said, 'On far off Ku She Mountain, there is a feminine spirit with flesh and bone like ice and snow, gentle and sweet as a virgin. She doesn't eat the Five Grains, but sips the breeze and the dew. She climbs the highest clouds and drives a chariot drawn by flying dragons, wandering the Four Seas at her leisure. Her spirit, when concentrated, keeps things from decaying and brings crops to fruition.' I thought him obviously mad, so gave his words no credence."

Lien Shu replied thoughtfully, "So. So it is indeed. The blind cannot know the beauty of emblem or artifice; the deaf cannot perceive the awesome sound of bell and drum. But how is it possible that deafness and blindness inhabit only flesh and bone? There is deafness and blindness in the comprehending mind as well. So it is with Chieh Yu's words. And yet there *is* this feminine spirit, this feminine principle that can bring ten thousand things into One. Our world, however, remains attached to disorder, everyone willing to accept All-under-heaven as their charge today. But this spirit lies beyond worldly harm. If waters should rise and flood the sky, she wouldn't drown; if the Great Drought returned, if mountains and hillsides ran with molten stone and iron, she wouldn't burn. You could smelt and cast sage emperors like Yao and Shun from the scraps and dust she leaves behind. Why would she wish to stoop to be in the service of mere things?"

∽

When Lao Tzu died, Chin Shih came to mourn. He uttered three loud cries and went out. A disciple said, "You're no friend of our master, are you?"

"I am so."

"If that's so, how can you mourn in this manner?"

"I mourn as I mourn," Chin Shih replied. "At first, I took *you* to be his men, but now I do not. When I went in to mourn, old folks were wailing as if for their own children and young folks wailing as if over their mothers. What is it that brought these people together? Certainly they have words to say and tears to cry that no one begged them for. But this is only hiding from true nature, turning one's back to actuality. In the old days, they called this 'hiding from the lessons of nature.'

"The master came, knowing his season. When it went, he followed. He is gone with his season, gone where he is supposed to go. Joys and sorrows cannot enter there. In the old days, this was called 'being cut free from bondage.'"

∞

Chuang Tzu's wife died, and when Hui Tzu came to offer his condolences, he found Chuang Tzu hunkered down, drumming on a pan and singing.

Hui Tzu said, "You lived with this woman, raised children with her, and grew old together. To not weep at her death is enough, already! But this drumming and singing, isn't this a bit too much?"

"No," Chuang Tzu replied. "That's not how it is. When she was first born into death, how could I have not felt grief? But I looked deeply into it and saw that before she was born into life, she was lifeless. Not only was she lifeless, but she was formless. Not only was she formless, she didn't even have any *ch'i*. Somewhere there in the vast imperceptible there was a change, and she had *ch'i*; then the *ch'i* changed, and she had form; the form changed, and she had life. Now there has been another change, and she is dead. This is like the mutual cycling of the four seasons. Now she lies resting quietly in the Great Chamber. If I were to go running in "Boo-hooing" after her, that would certainly show a failure to understand what is fated. So I stopped."

Translated with J. P. Seaton

Lu Chi
(CA. 261–300)

FROM THE ART OF WRITING

Preface

When studying the work of the masters,
    I watch the working of their minds.

Surely, facility with language
    and the charging of the word with energy

are effects which can be achieved
    by various means.

Still, the beautiful can be distinguished
    from the common,
    the good from the mediocre.

Only through writing and then revising
    and revising
    may one gain the necessary insight.

We worry whether our ideas
    may fall short of their subjects,
    whether form and content rhyme.

This may be easy to know,
    but it is difficult
    to put into practice.

I have composed this rhymed prose
    on the art of writing
    to introduce

past masterpieces
        as models for an examination
        of the good and the bad in writing.

Perhaps it will one day be said
        that I have written
        something of substance,

something useful,
        that I have entered
        the mystery.

When cutting an axe handle with an axe,
        surely the model is at hand.

Each writer finds a new entrance
        into the Mystery,
        and it is difficult to explain.

Nonetheless, I have set down my thinking
        as clearly as I can.

Beginning

Eyes closed, we listen
        to inner music,
        lost in thought and question:

Our spirits ride
        to the eight corners of the universe,
        mind soaring a thousand miles away;

only then may the inner voice
        grow clear
        as objects become numinous.

We pour forth
    the essence of words,
    savoring their sweetness.

It is like being adrift
    in a heavenly lake
    or diving to the depths of seas.

We bring up living words
    like fishes hooked in their gills,
    leaping from the deep.

Luminous words are brought down
    like birds on an arrow string
    shot from passing clouds.

We gather words and images
    from those unused
    by previous generations.

Our melodies
    have remained unplayed
    for a thousand years.

The morning blossoms bloom;
    soon, night buds will unfold.

Past and present commingle:
    Eternity
    in the single blink of an eye!

The Masterpiece

I take the rules of grammar
    and guides to good language

and clutch them
        to heart-and-mind.

Know what is
        and what is not
        merely fashion;

learn what old masters
        praised highly,

although the wisdom of a subtle mind
        is often scoffed at
        by the public.

The brilliant semi-precious stones
        of popular fashion
        are as common as beans in the field.

Though the writers
        of my generation
        produce in profusion,

all their real jewels
        cannot fill the little cup
        I make of my fingers.

As infinite as space, good work
        joins earth to heaven;

it comes from nothing,
        like air through a bellows.

We carry the bucket from the well,
        but the bucket soon is empty.

Wanting every word to sing,
        every writer worries:

nothing is ever perfected;
     no poet can afford to become complacent.

We hear a jade bell's laughter
     and think it laughs at us.

For a poet, there is terror in the dust.

WANG WEI
(701–761)

Return to Wang River

In the gorge where bells resound,
there are few fishermen or woodsmen.

Before I know it, dusk closes the mountains.
Alone, I return again to white clouds

and trembling water chestnuts
where willow catkins fly.

Spring grass colors the eastern landscape.
Snared in a web of grief, I close my wooden door.

Visiting the Mountain Hermitage of a Monk at Gan-hua Monastery

He waits at dusk, bamboo walking stick in hand,
at the headwaters of Tiger Creek,
leading us on as we listen to mountain echoes,
following the water's way.

Patches of wildflowers bloom.
A solitary bird calls from the valley floor.
We sit evening zazen in the empty forest:
quiet pine winds bring the scent of autumn.

The Way to the Temple

Searching for Gathered Fragrance Temple:
miles of mountains rise into clouds,
ancient trees darken the narrow trail.
Where is that mountain temple bell?

Snowmelt crashes down on boulders,
the sun grows cold in the pines before
it drowns in the lake. Keep your karma
in good working order: many dragons lie in wait.

Passing Hsiang-chi Temple

Oblivious, I pass Hsiang-chi Temple,
walking on through mountain clouds,
an empty trail through ancient trees.
Deep in the mountains, a bell resounds.

The susurrus river flows among stones.
Sunlight streams through frozen pines.
In this still pool, in falling light,
Zen overcomes the serpents of delusion.

Crossing the Yellow River

A little boat on the great river
whose waves reach the end of the sky—

suddenly a great city, ten thousand
houses dividing sky from wave.

Between the towns there are
hemp and mulberry trees in the wilds.

Look back on the old country:
wide waters; clouds; and rising mist.

A Meal for the Monks

I came late to the dharma,
but each day deepen my retreat.

Waiting for mountain monks,
I sweep my simple hut.

Then down from cloudy peaks
you come through knee-deep weeds.

We kneel on tatami, munching pine nuts.
We burn incense and study the Tao.

Light the lamp at twilight:
a single chime begins the night.

In every solitude, deep joy.
This life abides.

How can you think of returning?
A lifetime is empty like the void.

Li Po
(701–762)

About Tu Fu

I met Tu Fu on a mountaintop
in August when the sun was hot.

Under the shade of his big straw hat
his face was sad—

in the years since we'd last parted
he'd grown wan, exhausted.

Poor old Tu Fu, I thought then,
he must be agonizing over poetry again.

Saying Good-bye in a Ch'in-ling Wineshop

Spring winds perfume the shop
with heavy blooming catkins.

A girl from Wu pours wine
and encourages our drinking.

With friends from the city
I come to toast and say good-bye.

About to part, I point them toward
the great east-churning river.

Can any river possibly flow
beyond the love of friends?

Listening to a Flute in Yellow Crane Pavilion

I came here as a wanderer
    thinking of home,
remembering my faraway Ch'ang-an.

And then, from deep in Yellow Crane Pavilion,
    I heard a beautiful bamboo flute
play "Falling Plum Blossoms."

It was late summer in a city by a river.

Questions Answered

You ask why I live
alone in the mountain forest,

and I smile and am silent
until even my soul grows quiet.

The peach trees blossom.
The water continues to flow.

I live in the other world,
one that lies beyond the human.

Saying Good-bye to Meng Hao-jan at
Yellow Crane Pavilion

You said good-bye at Yellow Crane Pavilion
and sailed west, down into the valley
through the flowers and mists of spring

until your lonely sail vanished
in the blue sky's horizon,

and I was left watching the river
flowing gently into heaven.

Mountain Drinking Song

To drown the ancient sorrows,
we drank a hundred jugs of wine

there in beautiful moonlight. We couldn't
go to bed with the moon so bright.

Then finally the wine overcame us
and we lay down on the empty mountain:

earth for a pillow
and a blanket made of heaven.

Zazen on Ching-t'ing Mountain

The birds have vanished from the sky.
Now the last cloud drains away.

We sit together, the mountain and me,
until only the mountain remains.

Tu Fu
(712–770)

To Li Po on a Spring Day

There's no poet quite like you, Li Po,
you live in my imagination.

You sing as sweet as Yui,
and still retain Pao's nobility.

Under spring skies north of the Wei,
you wander into the sunset

toward the village of Chiang-tung.
Tell me, will we ever again

buy another keg of wine
and argue over prosody and rhyme?

The Draft Board at Shih-hao

As I was lodged at Shih-hao one night,
the draft board came for inductees.

While his wife delayed them at the gate,
one old man slipped over his wall and away.

The senior officer, in a rage,
cursed the woman into tears,

and then I heard her speak:
"All three of our sons went off to war.

And now a single letter returns—
two sons dead on the battlefield,

one on his last life's breath.
The dead are lost forever.

There's no one left at home
but a grandson nursing mother's breast,

too young to leave her side.
And she so poor her skirts are made of patches.

Although my strength has long since flown,
take *me* tonight, I beg you,

and I'll go to Ho-yang
and cook you all your breakfast."

The night and the voices passed,
except for the woman's sobbing.

I turned to the trail, first light breaking behind me
as the old man bid farewell to his family.

Clear After Rain

Long after rainfall, Sorceress Hills grow dark.
Now they brighten, stitched with gold and silver.

Green grass edges the darkening lake
and red clouds stream from the east.

All day long, the orioles call,
and cranes brush tall white clouds.

Once dry, the wildflowers bend and, there
where the wind is sweeping, fall.

Moon, Rain, Riverbank

Rain roared through, now
the autumn night is clear.
The water wears a patina of gold
and carries a bright jade star.
Heavenly River runs clear and pure,
as gently as before.

Sunset buries the mountains in shadow.
A mirror floats in the deep green void,
its light reflecting the cold, wet dusk,
dew glistening,
freezing on the flowers.

Night Thoughts While Traveling

Thin grass bends on the breezy shore,
and the tall mast seems lonely in my boat.

Stars wide low across the wide plain,
and the moon is tossed by the Yangtze.

What is fame and literary status?
The old and infirm should leave office.

Adrift, drifting: what is left for the lone gull
adrift between earth and heaven.

Heading South

Spring returns to Peach Blossom River
and my sail is a cloud through maple forests.

Exiled, I lived for years in secret, moving on
farther from home with tearstains on my sleeves.

Now old and sick, at last I'm headed south.
Remembering old friends, I look back north a final time.

A hundred years I sang my bitter song,
but not a soul remembers those old rhymes.

Yuan Chen
(779–831)

Letter Smuggled in a Fish

Your letter unfolds and unfolds forever.
I flatten it with my hands to read:

tearstains, tearstains and a trace of rouge
where it must have touched your cheek.

Peach Blossoms

Infinite peach-blossom shades,
her rouged and powdered cheeks.

Spring breezes help her break my heart,
blowing peach petals from her dress.

Elegy

Oh, loveliest daughter of Hsieh,
you married a hapless scholar
and spent your life with a needle,
patching his old clothes.

He thanked you by selling your gold pins
for wine. He picked herbs
and berries for your meals,
and locust leaves for the fire.

Now that they pay me handsomely,
there's no offering I can bring
but this sacrificial mourning.
We used to joke about dying.

Now you are suddenly gone.
I gave all your clothes away,
and packed up your needlework—
I couldn't bear to see them.

But I extend your kindness toward our maid,
and bring you gifts in lonely dreams.
Everyone learns this sorrow, but none
more than those who once suffered together.

Alone and lonely, I mourn for us both.
Approaching sixty, I know better men
who lived without a son, better poets
with dead wives who couldn't hear them.

In the dark of your tomb,
there is nothing left to hope for—
we had no faith in meeting after death.
Yet when I open my eyes,

I see through long nights
the grief that troubled your life.

Empty House

I leave my empty house at dawn
and ride to my empty office.

I fill the day with busywork.
At nightfall, back to my empty house.

Moonlight seeps through the cracks.
My wick has burned to ash.

My heart lies cold in Hsien-yang Road,
under the wheels of a hearse.

Su Tung-p'o
(1036–1101)

Climbing Yun-lung Mountain

Drunk, I scurry up a hillside
studded with sheep-sized boulders

until I stumble into a huge stone chair.
The sky is full of white clouds.

Autumn winds carry work songs
up from trails far below,

where workmen look up, astonished:
they clap their hands and yell.

Rain during the Cold Food Festival

This is my third Cold Food Festival
since I was exiled to Huang-chou.

Each parting spring, each year, I grieve.
Nevertheless, each passes—no regret.

This year there's pestilential rain,
the past two months dark as autumn.

I lie still, listening to cherry blossoms fall
into snow, pink and growing muddy.

Of what steals things in the dark,
the strangest arrives at midnight:

as though a young man went to bed
only to wake and find his hair turned white.

Remembering My Wife

Ten years ago, you died.
And my life ceased.

Even when I don't think of you,
I grieve. And with your grave

a thousand miles away,
there is no place for me

to give my grief a voice.
You wouldn't know me

if you saw me now,
me with snowy hair and a dusty face.

I dreamed myself home last night,
and saw you through a window

as you combed out your hair.
When you saw me, we were speechless

until we burst into silent tears.
Year after year, I remember

that moonlit night we spent alone
together in hills of stunted pine.

Li Ch'ing-chao
(1084–1151)

Plum Blossoms

The fragrance of red lotuses has faded.
Autumn settles at my door.

I loosen my robe and drift in an orchid boat.
Someone sent me love notes in the clouds,

in lines of returning geese,
in moonlight flooding the pavilion.

Flowers fade alone. Rivers flow alone.
Only our longing is shared.

Sadness, grief, and worry
grow heavy in my eyes,

we are so long apart—
and settle in the bottom of my heart.

Spring at Wu Ling

The breeze has passed,
     pollen dust settled,
and now the evening comes
     as I comb out my hair.

There is the book, the inkstone, the table.
     But he who was my life

is gone. It is difficult
        to speak through tears.

I've heard it's always spring
        at Wu Ling, and beautiful.
I'd take a little boat and drift
        alone out on the water.

But I'm afraid a boat
        so small would swamp
with the weight
        of all my sorrows.

Eternal Joy

Sunset pours its gold through jade-colored clouds.
But he has gone and heavy mist obliterates the willows.

Someone plays "Falling Plum Blossoms" on a flute,
and spring sadly passes.

The Lantern Festival signals calmer weather,
but tomorrow brings winds and rain.

My friend sends a horse and carriage, but I can't bear
the company of old poetry-and-wine companions.

Long ago, in women's quarters, we celebrated
festivals all night in belts and necklaces of gold,

with emeralds in our hair—each outshining the other.
Now frail, windblown, and gray, I won't brave

an evening garden walk among those flowery girls—
I'll remain behind drawn curtains,

eavesdropping, old—
listening to the heartbreak of their joy.

Sands of the Washing Stream

Beyond barred windows,
shadows cover the garden,

shadows slide over the curtain
as I play my lute in silence.

Distant mountains stretch the sunset,
breezes bring clouds and rain.

The pear blossoms fade and die,
and I can't keep them from falling.

Boat of Stars

Spring after spring, I sat before my mirror.
Now I tire of braiding plum buds in my hair.

I've gone another year without you,
shuddering with each letter—

since you've been gone,
even wine has lost its flavor.

I wept until it was autumn,
my thoughts going south beside you.

Even the gates of heaven
are nearer to me now than you.

✻ *Japanese Poets*

Saigyō
(1118–1190)

With an empty heart
I left society. How
deeply moved I am
when a snipe bursts from the field
in the autumn evening.

No one visits here
in my mountain hut
where I live alone.
But for this sweet loneliness,
it would be too much to bear.

He whose heart and soul
are at one with the great void
steps into the mist
and suddenly thinks himself
stepping right out of this world.

Even among those
who think themselves indifferent

toward most things,
it brings an inner shiver—
this first cool autumn wind.

Touring Kisagata by Boat

In Kisagata,
the flowering cherry trees
vanish under waves—
until an old fisherman
rows out across blossoms.

On the clear mirror,
just a single speck of dust.
And yet we see it
before all else, our poor world
having come to what it is.

Dead, I'll lie forever
alone beneath a blanket
of cold moss
remembering what is learned
only from dew and dark stone.

If possible,
I hope to be beneath
those last cherry blossoms
when I die—right around the time
of the full moon of spring.

The mind is all sky,
the heart utterly empty,
and the perfect moon
is completely transparent
entering western mountains.

Ikkyū
(1394–1481)

Song of the Dream Garden

Pillowed on your thighs in a dream garden,
little flower with its perfumed stamen,

singing, sipping from the stream of you—
Sunset. Moonlight. Our song continues.

∞

Face to Face with My Lover on Daito's Anniversary

Monks recite the sutras in honor of the Founder,
their many voices cacophonous in my ear.

Afterward, making love, our intimate whispers
mock the empty formal discipline of others.

∞

My hand is Lady Mori's hand
and knows her mastery of love.

When I am weak, she resurrects my jeweled stem.
The monks I train are grateful then.

∞

Elegy

We first lay down among flowers
ten years ago and found a timeless rapture.

Sadly, I remember being pillowed by her lap,
all-night love, all eternity in our vows.

Without beginning,
utterly without end,
the mind is born
to struggles and distresses,
and dies—and that is emptiness.

Like vanishing dew,
a passing apparition
or the sudden flash
of lightning—already gone—
thus should one regard one's self.

The moon is a house
in which the mind is master.
Look very closely:
only impermanence lasts.
This floating world too will pass.

And what is mind
and how is it recognized?
It is clearly drawn
in sumi ink, the sound
of breezes drifting through pine.

Bashō
(1644–1694)

The moon and sun are eternal travelers.* Even the years wander on. A lifetime adrift in a boat, or in old age leading a tired horse into the years, every day is a journey, and the journey itself is home. From the earliest times there have always been some who perished along the road.† Still I have always been drawn by windblown clouds into dreams of a lifetime of wandering. Coming home from a year's walking tour of the coast last autumn, I swept the cobwebs from my hut on the banks of the Sumida just in time for New Year, but by the time spring mists began to rise from the fields, I longed to cross the Shirakawa Barrier into the Northern Interior. Drawn by the wanderer-spirit Dosojin, I couldn't concentrate on things. Mending my cotton pants, sewing a new strap on my bamboo hat, I daydreamed. Rubbing moxa into my legs to strengthen them, I dreamed a bright moon rising over Matsushima. So I placed my house in another's hands and moved to my patron Mr. Sampu's summer house in preparation for my journey. And I left a verse by my door:

> Even this grass hut
> may be transformed
> into a doll's house‡

∞

Very early on the twenty-seventh morning of the third moon, under a predawn haze, transparent moon still visible,§ Mount. Fuji just a shadow,

---

*Echoes the famous preface of a poem ("Peach Garden Banquet on a Spring Night") by the T'ang dynasty poet Li Po.
†Bashō is thinking of the T'ang poet Tu Fu (712–770) and the wandering monk Saigyō (1118–1190).
‡Refers to *Hina Matsuri*, Girls' Festival, comparing his tiny thatched hut to his patron's mansion.
§An allusion to *Tale of Genji*.

I set out under the cherry blossoms of Ueno and Yanaka. When would I see them again? A few old friends had gathered in the night and followed along far enough to see me off from the boat. Getting off at Senju, I felt three thousand miles rushing through my heart, the whole world only a dream. I saw it through farewell tears.

> Spring passes
> and the birds cry out—tears
> in the eyes of fishes

With these first words from my brush, I started. Those who remain behind watch the shadow of a traveler's back disappear.

Set out to see the Murder Stone, Sessho-seki, on a borrowed horse, and the man leading it asked for a poem, "Something beautiful, please."

> The horse turns his head—
> from across the wide plain,
> a cuckoo's cry

Sessho-seki lies in dark mountain shadow near a hot springs emitting bad gasses. Dead bees and butterflies cover the sand.

Here three generations of the Fujiwara clan passed as though in a dream. The great outer gates lay in ruins. Where Hidehira's manor stood, rice fields grew. Only Mount Kinkei remained. I climbed the hill where Yoshitsune died; I saw the Kitakami, a broad stream flowing down through the Nambu Plain, the Koromo River circling Izumi Castle below the hill before joining the Kitakami. The ancient ruins of Yasuhira—from the end of the Golden Era—lie out beyond the Koromo Barrier where they stood guard against the Ainu people. The faithful elite remained bound to the castle, for all their valor, reduced to ordinary grass. Tu Fu wrote:

The whole country devastated
only mountains and rivers remain.
In springtime, at the ruined castle,
the grass is always green.

We sat a while, our hats for a seat, seeing it all through tears.

Summer grasses:
all that remains of great soldiers'
imperial dreams

The road through the Nambu Plain visible in the distance, we stayed the night in Iwate, then trudged on past Cape Oguro and Mizu Island, both along the river. Beyond Narugo Hot Springs, we crossed Shito-mae Barrier and entered Dewa Province. Almost no one comes this way, and the barrier guards were suspicious, slow, and thorough. Delayed, we climbed a steep mountain in falling dark, and took refuge in a guardshack. A heavy storm pounded the shack with wind and rain for three miserable days.

Eaten alive by
lice and fleas—now the horse
beside my pillow pees

In Yamagata Province, the ancient temple founded by Jikaku Daishi in 860, Ryūshaku Temple is stone quiet, perfectly tidy. Everyone told us to see it. It meant a few miles extra, doubling back toward Obanazawa to find shelter. Monks at the foot of the mountain offered rooms, then we climbed the ridge to the temple, scrambling up through ancient gnarled pine and oak, gray smooth stones and moss. The temple doors, built on rocks, were bolted. I crawled among boulders to make my bows at shrines. The silence was profound. I sat, feeling my heart begin to open.

Lonely stillness—
a single cicada's cry
sinking into stone

At a village called Komatsu:

Aptly named Komatsu,
Child Pine, a breeze blows over
pampas and clover

Here we visited Tada Shrine to see Sanemori's* helmet and a piece
of his brocade armor-cloth presented to him by Lord Yoshitomo when
he served the Genji clan. His helmet was no common soldier's gear:
engraved with chrysanthemums and ivy from eye-hole to ear-flap,
crowned with a dragon's head between two horns. After Sanemori died
on the battlefield, Kiso Yoshinaka sent it with a prayer, hand-carried
to the shrine by Higuchi Jirō, Sanemori's friend. The story's inscribed
on the shrine.

Pitifully—under
a great soldier's empty helmet,
a cricket sings

---

*Sanemori's tale is told in *Heike Monogatari*, in *Genpei seisuiki*, and in a Noh play by
Zeami, *Sanemori*.

Within this temporal body composed of a hundred bones and nine holes there resides a spirit which, for lack of an adequate name, I think of as windblown. Like delicate drapery, it may be torn away and blown off by the least breeze. It brought me to writing poetry many years ago, initially for its own gratification, but eventually as a way of life. True, frustration and rejection were almost enough to bring this spirit to silence, and sometimes pride brought it to the brink of vanity. From the writing of the very first line, it has found no contentment as it was torn by one doubt after another. This windblown spirit considered the security of court life at one point; at another, it considered risking a display of its ignorance by becoming a scholar. But its passion for poetry would not permit either. Since it knows no other way than the way of poetry, it has clung to it tenaciously.

Saigyō in poetry, Sōgi in linked verse, Sesshū in painting, Rikyū in the tea ceremony—the spirit that moves them is one spirit. Achieving artistic excellence, each holds one attribute in common: each remains attuned to nature throughout the four seasons. Whatever is seen by such a heart and mind is a flower, whatever is dreamed is a moon. Only a barbarian mind could fail to see the flower; only an animal mind could fail to dream a moon. The first task for each artist is to overcome the barbarian or animal heart and mind, to become one with nature.

Selected Haiku

Between our two lives
there is also the life of
the cherry blossom

Under full blossom—
a spirited monk and
a flirtatious wife

Culture's beginnings:
from the heart of the country,
rice planting songs

How very noble!
One who finds no satori
in the lightning-flash

On a bare branch,
a solitary crow—
autumn evening

At the ancient pond
a frog plunges into
the sound of water

Nothing in the cry
of cicadas suggests they
are about to die

The bee emerging
from deep within the peony
departs reluctantly

A trapped octopus—
one night of dreaming
with the summer moon

I slept at a temple—
and now with such seriousness
I watch the moon

With clear melting dew,
I'd try to wash away the dust
of this floating world

On a Portrait of Hotei, God of Good Fortune

How much I desire!
Inside my little satchel,
the moon and flowers

BUSON
(1715–1783)

Priestly poverty—
he carves a wooden Buddha
through a long cold night

Clinging to the bell,
he dozes so peacefully,
this new butterfly

The camellia tips,
the remains of last night's rain
splashing out

With no under-robes,
bare butt suddenly exposed—
a gust of spring wind

Sweet springtime showers,
and no words can express
how sad it all is

Head pillowed on arm,
such affection for myself!
and this smoky moon

The late evening crow
of deep autumn longing
suddenly cries out

In a bitter wind
a solitary monk bends
to words cut in stone

This cold winter night,
that old wooden-head Buddha
would make a nice fire

Nobly, the great priest
deposits his daily stool
in bleak winter fields

RYŌKAN
(1758–1831)

Who says my poems are poems?
They aren't poems at all.

Only when you understand my poems aren't poems
can we talk poetry.

In my hut, I keep *Han Shan's Poems*.
They're better than any sutra.

I copy out his poems and pin them up
and recite them again and again.

(Poem in Four Characters)

Above Heaven
big winds

Too stupid to live among men,
I pass my years among herbs and trees;

too lazy to learn right from wrong,
laugh at me and I laugh along.

These old bones still cross the river,
begging-bag in hand, loving springtime weather.

I manage to survive.
I never once despised this world.

∞

You stop to point at the moon in the sky,
but the finger's blind unless the moon is shining.

One moon, one careless finger pointing—
are these two things or one?

The question is a pointer guiding
a novice from ignorance thick as fog.

Look deeper. The mystery calls and calls:
No moon, no finger—nothing there at all.

∞

The winds have died, but flowers go on falling;
birds call, but silence penetrates each song.

The Mystery! Unknowable, unlearnable.
The virtue of Kannon.

∞

Illusion and enlightenment are mutually entangled;
means and end, cause and effect are one.

Dawn to dusk I study worldless texts in silence;
nights are lost to thoughtless meditation.

Warblers sing in the willows.
Dogs bark late in the moonlit village.

All emotions rise in a whirl.
I leave this old heart to the world.

Was it all a dream—
I mean those old bygone days—
were they what they seemed?
All night long I lie awake
listening to autumn rain.

What might I leave you
as my lasting legacy—
flowers in springtime,
the cuckoo singing all summer,
yellow maple leaves of autumn.

Issa

(1763–1827)

FROM THE SPRING OF MY LIFE

Still clothed in the dust of this suffering world, I celebrate the first day in my own way. And yet I am like the priest, for I too shun trite popular seasonal congratulations. The commonplace "crane" and "tortoise" echo like empty words, like the actors who come begging on New Year's Eve with empty wishes for prosperity. The customary New Year pine will not stand beside my door. I won't even sweep my dusty house, living as I do in a tiny hermitage constantly threatening to collapse under harsh north winds. I leave it all to the Buddha, as in the ancient story.

The way ahead may be dangerous, steep as snowy trails winding through high mountains. Nevertheless I welcome the New Year just as I am.

> New Year greeting-time:
> I feel about average
> welcoming my spring

∞

> Written on Buddha's Death Day [March 15, 1819]:

> Aloof and silent
> like the Buddha, I lie still—
> still troubled by flowers

∞

On a beautiful spring morning, a young monk-in-training named Taka-maru, still a child at eleven, left Myosen Temple with a big monk named Kanryō. They planned to pick herbs and flowers in Araizaka, but the boy slipped on an old bridge and plunged into the icy, roaring river, which was swollen with snowmelt and runoff from Iizuna Mountain.

Hearing the boy's screams for help, Kanryō dashed down the bank, but there was nothing he could do. Takamaru's head bobbed up, then disappeared. A hand rose above the raging water. But soon his cries grew as faint as the high buzz of mosquitoes, and the young monk vanished in the river, nothing left but his image engraved forever on Kanryō's eyes.

On into the evening, torches flared along the bank as people searched for Takamaru. Finally, he was found, his body wedged between boulders, too late for anyone to help.

When someone found a handful of young butterburs in the dead boy's pocket, probably a gift for his parents, even those who seldom weep began to soak their sleeves. They lifted his body onto a bamboo palanquin and carried him home.

It was late evening when his parents ran out to see his body, their bitter tears observed by everyone. True, as followers of the Way, they had always preached transcendence of this life's miseries, but who could act otherwise? Their all-too-human hearts were shattered by undying love for their child. When the boy had left at dawn, he had been alive and laughing.

The young monk lay still and cold in the evening. Two days later, joining the funeral procession at his cremation, I wrote this tanka:

> Not once did I think
> I'd throw these fresh spring blossoms
> into this dense smoke
> and stand back to watch it rise
> and vanish into the sky.

As much as Takamaru's parents, flowers too must weep to know they may be hacked down and burned on any day just as they open their faces to warm spring sun after months of winter snow. Don't flowers have a life? Won't they, as much as we, realize nirvana in the end?

∞

Several people told me a story about some folks who heard heavenly music at two in the morning on New Year's Day. Furthermore, they all said, these people have heard it again every eighth day since. They described exactly when and where each hearing occurred.

Some people laughed it off as the trickeries of the wind, but I was reluctant to accept or dismiss the story without evidence. Heaven and earth are home to many mysteries. We all know the stories of dancing girls who pour the morning dew from high above. Perhaps the spirits who observe from the corridors of the heavens, seeing a peaceful world, called for music to rejoice. And perhaps we who failed to hear it were deafened by our own suffering.

I invited a few friends to visit my hermitage the morning of March 19th, and we spent the whole night listening. By the time first light broke in the east, we'd heard nothing. Then, suddenly, we heard singing from the plum tree outside a window.

> Just a bush warbler
> to sing morning Lotus Sutra
> to this suffering world

After an illness:

> I, too, made of dust—
> thin and light as the paper
> mosquito curtain

In Susaka Township in Shinano Province, a certain Dr. Nakamura, with capricious nastiness, killed a pair of snakes as they were mating. Late that night he was so overcome with searing pain in his penis that it rotted and fell off and he died.

The doctor's son, Santetsu, followed in his father's profession. He was a big man with an enormous mushroom-shaped penis. On his wedding night, however, he was dismayed to find it hanging useless, soft and thin as a candlewick. Overcome with shame, he sought other women, as many as a hundred, hoping to make it with them in order to recover, but always with the same embarrassing result, until he eventually sought refuge in seclusion.

Until I heard this story, I'd never been interested in tales of the supernatural, thinking them no more than regional folktales popularized in old anthologies. But this story prompted me to consider the vengeance of snakes and how the family suffered in turn.

All sentient beings are given life, even fleas and lice, and life is equally dear to each. It is bad enough to kill, but to kill them while they are in the act of procreation is truly terrible.

Kōsetsu wrote:

> I'd love to slap that
> fly on the beautiful face
> of my young stepchild

Last summer, at bamboo planting time, my wife gave birth to our daughter, whom we named Sato. Born in ignorance, we hoped she would grow in wisdom. On her birthday this year she whirled her arms and head for us and cried. We thought she was asking for a paper windmill, so I bought her one. She tried licking it, then sucking on it, then simply tossed it aside.

Her mind wanders from one thing to the next, never alighting very long on anything. One moment playing with a clay pot, in the next she shatters it. She examines a shōji screen, only to rip it open. When we sing her praises, her face lights up. Not a single dark cloud seems to have crossed her mind. She beams like clear moonlight, far more entertaining than the best stage act. When a passerby asks her to point out a dog or bird, she performs with her whole body, head to toe, poised like a butterfly on a grass blade, resting her wings.

She lives in a state of grace. The divine Buddha watches over her. On our annual evening honoring the dead, she comes crawling out as I light the candles on the family altar and ring the prayer bell. She folds her little hands, bending them like bracken shoots, and recites her prayer in a high, sweet voice.

I am old enough for frosty hair, the years add wrinkles to my face. I've not yet found Buddha's grace myself. I've wasted days and nights in empty busyness. It shames me to realize that my daughter, two years old, is closer to Buddhahood than I. But the moment I turn from the altar, I engage in bad karma, despising flies that crawl across my skin, swatting mosquitoes as they buzz about the table, or—worse—drinking wine, which is forbidden by the Buddha.

In the midst of my confession, moonlight falls over the gate like a cool breath. A group of dancing children suddenly begins to sing. My daughter drops her bowl and crawls out on the porch and joins her voice to the others, lifting her hands to the moon. Watching, I forget my advancing age and worldly ways. I daydream about a time when she'll be old enough for long waves of hair, when we encourage her to dance. Surely she could outshine the music of two dozen heavenly maidens. Day in, day out, her legs never rest. By nightfall, she's exhausted and sleeps deeply until the sun is high. While she sleeps, her mother cooks and cleans. Only then can her mother find a moment's rest before she awakens again with a cry. Her mother carries her out to the yard to pee, then nurses her. Our daughter sucks with a smile, poking the breast happily. Her mother then forgets the weariness and pain of having carried her in the womb, she forgets the dirty diapers she washes every day, lost in the supreme joy of having such a child, more precious than jewels.

> Nursing, mother counts
> the fleabites on her daughter's
> small white body

It is often said that the greatest pleasures result in the greatest misery. But why is it that my little child, who's had no chance to savor even half the world's pleasures—who should be green as new needles on the eternal pine—why should she be found on her deathbed, puffy with blisters raised by the despicable god of smallpox? How can I, her father, stand by and watch her fade away each day like a perfect flower suddenly ravaged by rain and mud?

Two or three days later, her blisters dried to hard scabs and fell off like dirt softened by melting snow. Encouraged, we made a tiny boat of straw and poured hot saké over it with a prayer and sent it floating downriver in hopes of placating the god of the pox. But our hope and efforts were useless and she grew weaker day by day. Finally, at midsummer, as the morning glory flowers were closing, her eyes closed forever.

Her mother clutched her cold body and wailed. I knew her heartbreak but also knew that tears were useless, that water under the bridge never returns, that scattered flowers are gone forever. And yet nothing I could do would cut the bonds of human love.

> This world of dew
> is only the world of dew—
> and yet . . . oh and yet . . .

Visiting my daughter's grave on July 25th, one month after her death:

> The red flower
> you always wanted to pick—
> now this autumn wind

Selected Haiku

He glares back at me
with an ugly, surly face,
this old pond frog

Summer's first melon
lies firmly hugged to the breast
of a sleeping child

Hurry now, my flies!
You too may share the riches
of this fine harvest

Even the flies
in the village of my birth
draw blood with each bite

The old woman
wiped her nose on the blossom
of a moonflower

My home is so poor
even the resident flies
keep their family small

Lying in hammocks,
we speak so solemnly of
distant thunder, distant rain

"Wolf scat!" Just the words
are enough to send icy
shivers down my spine

With just the slightest
parting of my lips, thousands
of plovers take flight

Be calm, skinny frog!
Now that Issa's on his way,
you needn't worry

In my hermitage
winter poverty drives me
to eat many strange things

So much money made
by clever temple priests
using peonies

All around my house,
pond frogs, from the beginning,
sang about old age

Here in Shinano
are famous moons, and buddhas,
and our good noodles

The distant mountains
are reflected in the eye
of the dragonfly

I wish she were here
to listen to my bitching
and enjoy this moon

The old dog listens
intently, as if to the
work songs of the worms

After a long nap,
the cat yawns, rises, and goes out
looking for love

Don't kill that poor fly!
He cowers, wringing
his hands for mercy

From the Great Buddha's
great nose, a swallow comes
gliding out

Give me a homeland,
and a passionate woman,
and winter alone

A world of dew,
and within every dewdrop
a world of struggle

In the midst of this world
we stroll along the roof of hell
gawking at flowers

Loneliness already
planted with each seed in
morning glory beds

From birthing's washbowl
to the washbowl of the dead—
blathering nonsense

Yosano Akiko
(1878–1942)

Gently, I open
the door to eternal
mystery, the flowers
of my breasts cupped,
offered with both hands.

I whisper, "Good night,"
slipping silently from his room
in the spring evening,
and pause at his kimono,
and try it on for size.

What can I put in
my burning mouth now the blood
from my lover's finger—
he asked me to kiss it—
begins to dry on my lips?

In return for all
the sins and crimes of men,
the gods created me
with glistening long black hair
and pale, inviting skin.

My shining black hair
fallen into disarray,
a thousand tangles,
like a thousand tangled thoughts
about my love for you.

Hair in morning tangles,
perhaps I should comb it out
with spring rainwater
as it drips from the ink-black
feathers of swallows' wings.

All alone
beside the temple bell:
I stole away
to secretly meet you here.
But now the fog has cleared.

Mountain Moving Day

"Mountain moving day has come,"
is what I say. But no one believes it.
Mountains were just sleeping for awhile.
Earlier, they had moved, burning with fire.
But you do not have to believe it.
O people! You'd better believe it!
All the sleeping women move
now that they awaken.

Self Awareness

From the day when, after saying inadvertently,
"I have decided to die,"
I saw a shaking man, surprised and pale,
my desire to die completely disappeared.
To tell you the truth, from that day
I came to know my world.

✣ Jaan Kaplinski
(B. 1941)

The house silent
water dripping
from a rinsed diaper
into the empty basin
everybody already asleep

I forgot
a short poem that
came into my mind
sitting in the rocking chair
with my little daughter
in my lap

I did not dare
to take a pencil
and write it down
feeling this silence
and the sleeping child
has a meaning
deeper than words

New butterflies are made of dust and color, but we
are planted in the ground like broken bones to replace ourselves.
Somewhere in storm and darkness, waves lap newborn islands
    like the lioness licks her cubs.
Words take their first steps on the darkness of white pages
    where there are no shadows, no depths, no distances

until something utterly new is born co-ordinate with Aurora Borealis
    and silver-starred hammer-blows fall through deep sleep,
walls touch fingers and syrup hums in the maple's virgin heart.
Once we were to meet our children's, our parents' blood.
    Red strawberries stretch out their hands and geraniums are
        strangely silent.
Dunes grow here as if white sand remembered the murmur
    of the rivers of paradise. Lone ants lose themselves in the
        wind, carnations
blaze up on beaches, something burns unavoidably, and night sleeps
    in the moor's warm lap while nearby star clusters break in
        its hair.
Fleet memory filled with ancient waterfall roars, seashells,
    and bees asleep behind dark walls—
will anything be reborn? Everything burns deep, deep,
    coals blanch and arteries harden,
and when the time comes to rise, ashes won't let go of our hands,
    wing-feathered spring fog freezes.
How does the child's smile lose itself in the king's chamber,
    where does clover, that four-leafed fortune, find courage to grow
    beneath these forbidding pillars
when even the black inscriptions on the birches fade and the leaves'
        green flight
    wearies before clay becomes clay and the bloody mud sinks
        back into soil?
No, no one anywhere needs your history, your ends and beginnings.
Peace. Simple peace to the jellyfish, and to grouse eggs; peace,
    to the ant's pathways; peace, to birds of paradise and to the ginko
    peace, to the sky; peace, to you snipe's flight
peace, to apples, pears, plums, apricots, oranges,
    wild roses growing on the railroad guardshack:
Requiem, Requiem aeterum.

∞

The East-West border is always wandering,
sometimes eastward, sometimes west,

75

and we do not know exactly where it is just now:
in Gaugemela, in the Urals, or maybe in ourselves,
so that one ear, one eye, one nostril, one hand, one foot
one lung and one testicle or one ovary
is on the one, another on the other side. Only the heart,
only the heart is always on one side:
if we are looking northward, in the West;
if we are looking southward, in the East;
and the mouth doesn't know on behalf of which or both
it has to speak.

We started home, my son and I.
Twilight already. The young moon
stood in the western sky and beside it
a single star. I showed them to my son
and explained how the moon should be greeted
and that this star is the moon's servant.
As we neared home, he said
that the moon is far, as far
as that place where we went.
I told him the moon is much, much farther
and reckoned: if one were to walk
ten kilometers each day, it would take
almost a hundred years to reach the moon.
But this was not what he wanted to hear.
The road was already almost dry.
The river was spread on the marsh; ducks and other waterfowl
crowed the beginning of night. The snow's crust
crackled underfoot—it must
have been freezing again. All the houses' windows
were dark. Only in our kitchen
a light shone. Beside our chimney, the shining moon,
and beside the moon, a single star.

Once I got a postcard from the Fiji Islands
with a picture of sugar cane harvest. Then I realized
that nothing at all is exotic in itself.
There is no difference between digging potatoes in our Mutiku garden
and sugar cane harvesting in Viti Levu.
Everything that is is very ordinary
or, rather, neither ordinary nor strange.
Far-off lands and foreign peoples are a dream,
a dreaming with open eyes
somebody does not wake from.
It's the same with poetry—seen from afar
it's something special, mysterious, festive.
No, poetry is even less
special than a sugar cane plantation or potato field.
Poetry is like sawdust coming from under the saw
or soft yellowish shavings from a plane.
Poetry is washing hands in the evening
or a clean handkerchief that my late aunt
never forgot to put in my pocket.

It gets cold in the evening. The sky clears.
The wind dies out, and the smoke
rises straight up. The flowering maple
no longer buzzes. A carp
plops in the pond. An owl hoots twice
in its nest in the ash tree.
The children are asleep. On the stairs,
a long row of shoes and rubber boots.
It happened near Viljandi: an imbecile boy
poured gasoline on the neighbor's three-year-old son
and set him on fire. I ran for milk.
You could see the yellow maple from far off

between the birches and the spruce. The evening star
was shining above the storehouse. The boy survived,
probably maimed for life. The night will bring frost.
Plentiful dew.

Sometimes I see so clearly the openness of things.
The teapot has no lid, the colt has no saddle.
Black horses come racing out of memory
carrying young boys on their backs and rush over
the empty steppe and through the haze
through which we see, dimly,
some single peaks. . . . I too have come from there.
I have something of you, my forefathers,
Amurat, Ahmed, Tokhtash, something of you
black Tartar horses on boundless expanses.
I too do not like to return
to lived life, to an extinguished fire,
to a thought thought to a written poem.
I am burning with the same urge to reach the Atlantic,
to reach the borders always vanishing and breaking
in front of the black horses who again and again
race out from memories and steppes
smelling the west wind that brings from somewhere very far
the odor of the sea and rain.

Almost Paradise

New and Selected Poems

The Nets

Somewhere someone is untangling
the heavy nets of desire
beside a small fire at the edge of the sea.

He works slowly, fingers bleeding,
half thinking, half listening, knowing
only that the sea makes him thirsty.

A Lover's Quarrel

There are some to whom a place means nothing,
for whom the lazy zeroes
a goshawk carves across the sky
are nothing,
for whom a home is something one can buy.
I have long wanted to say,
just once before I die,
I am home.

When I remember the sound of my true country,
I hear winds
high up in the evergreens, the soft snore
of surf, far off, on a wintry day,
the half-garbled song of finches
darting off through alder
on a summer day.

Lust does not
fatigue the soul, I say. This wind,

these ever-
green trees, this little bird of the spirit—
this is the shape, the place of my desire. I'm free
as a fish or a stone.

　　　•

Don't tell me
about the seasons in the East, don't talk to me
about eternal California summer.
It's enough to have
a few days naked
among three hundred kinds of rain.

In its little plastic pot on the high sill,
the African violet
grows away from the place
the sun last was, its fuzzy leaves
leaning out in little curtsies.

It, too, has had enough
of the sun. I love the sound of a storm
without thunder, the way winds
slow, trees darken, heavy clouds
rumbling so softly
you must close your eyes to listen:

then the *blotch, blotch*
of big drops
plunketing through the leaves.

　　　•

It is difficult,
this being a stranger on earth.
Why, I've seen pilgrims come

and tear away at blackberry vines
with everything that's in them, I've seen them
heap their anger
up against a tree
and curse these swollen skies.

What's this?—a mountain beaver
no bigger than a newborn mouse
curled in my palm,
an osprey curling over tide pools and lifting
toward the trees, a wind at dusk
hollow in the hollows of the eves,
a wind over waves
cooling sand crabs washed up along the beach.

Each thing, closely seen,
appears more strange
than before: the shape of my desire
is huge, vague,
full of many things
commingling—

dying bees among the dying flowers;
winter rain and the smoke it brings.

If it fills me with longing,
it is only because
we are like the rain, falling,
falling through our own most secret being,
through a world of not-knowing.

•

At the end of the day,
I come, finally,
to myself, I return to the strange sounds of a man
who wants to speak

with stones, with the hard crust of earth.
But nothing listens.

When the sea hammers the sea wall,
I'm dumb.
When the nighthawks bleat at dusk, I'm drunk
on the sadness of their songs.
When the moon is so close
you can almost reach it through the trees,
I'm frozen, I'm blind,
or I'm gone.

Fish, bird, stone, there's something
I can't know, but know the same:
I hear the rain inside me
only to look up
into a bitter sun.

What do we listen to, what do we think
we hear? The sound
of sea walls crumbling,
a little bird with hunger in its song:
You should have known! You should have known!

•

Like any Nootka rose,
I know there are some
for whom a place is nothing. Like the wild rose,
like the tide and the day,
we come, go, or stay
according to a whim.

It is enough, perhaps,
to say, *We live here.*
And let it go at that.

This wind lets go
of everything it touches.
I long to hold the wind.

I'd kiss a fish
and love a stone
and marry this winter rain

if I could persuade this battered earth
to let me make it home.

Gnostology

Each return is a blessing,
a birthing. I come back again
in the last light of evening and the blue cups
camas raises to catch the mist
are dripping, blackberries turning blue from green,
and down the narrow Strait of Juan de Fuca,
foghorns faintly sound.

I stand a long time outside, listening
to the dripping leaves and nighthawk cries.
Behind me, the dark house drips from the eaves.
I slide the wide door open to scents
of stale beer and cigarettes
I smoked last week.

The same books clutter the table.
The same poem dies
in the crude last unfinished line.
I ease into my tattered chair
in trembling light
as the sunset slides into a shadow
ghosting the dark Pacific.

Somewhere, the tide is staggering
over stones at the feet of incoming swells;
the gulls are scavenging, looping
a last time over brine, searching for edibles
tangled in the wrack.
The moon slips between two cedars,
razor thin and curved into
a dazzling sliver of ice
simmering in the fog.
The dark of night settles in
on strong, steady feet.

This silence is not
profound—it's an old friend, my beautiful
dark daughter I haven't seen in years,
a longing, a soft exquisite ache.
An hour flies. Another. This life's
a summer reverie, a dream
flashing past unnoticed
at the edge of sleep,
a simple gesture—a touch
or kiss of a friend.

Finally, I rise
and step out of my clothes
and stand on the porch in the mist,
suddenly naked, lightly goose-fleshed,
more alive than I have been
in days. My whole body
responds to mist and air, the moist touch
of evening bristling hairs of belly
and legs, and I feel my nipples' erection,
my scrotum draw up against my groin, my toes
count every grain of earth beneath my feet.

Out in the blank space of night, thousands
and thousands of systems are at work—

lighting galaxies, whirling the billions
of years into a ball.

Are
the ants asleep inside their catacombs of fir?
Are the chloroplasts resting their eyes?
With no prayer on my breath, without
hope or fear, without asking what it is
or what the seasons know,
I gather a long, slow breath, kneel,
and bow.

A Cold Fire

An hour after sunset, Venus hangs
in the wintry mist of the west,
a cold fire burning alone above wet trees
and hills that fall and rise through fog.

We stand together a long time
hand in hand, watching
what we each have watched
a thousand times before.

Darkness and silence join hands
and spread over us the cool caress
of their breath. There is nothing
to say, nothing to do.

Startled into being something we'd
only dreamed of being,
we enter the exquisite abyss
of the first hour before heaven.

To Kevin, Who Mourns

In memoriam, Jay Sisson

We watch the weather unloading all its wares:
gray clouds, cold rain, winds no one dares
to brave. The deep woods where Jaybird fell
are silent, or they groan into shadows that swell
into a dark too deep to penetrate, too dense
to let a life escape. He died. What sense
we make of it or do not make, we feel
somehow betrayed, hurt or shamed. We kneel
beside a grave and weep for our own ensuing years
of solitude before the vague death we fear
grows friendly and familiar and the pain
of remembered deaths grows dim, a slight stain
spotting someone else's linen, we recall,
in the April of our years before the fall
winds blew the old gaunt Salesman in
to spread before us the wooden cross and tin
Jesus in his pain. We cannot buy the dead
another life. And yet we make them live, fed
by love, work, memory we freely give,
nourished by the weather of the lives we live.

To John Logan from La Push

These heaped-up, half-paved streets
are no man's heaven, least of all
a drunk's. Stoked on wine
and brimming with regrets,
landlocked sailors swill their brew
below their rotting decks:
they dream tuna, money, and honey-haired girls
and fish from wreck to wreck.

You saw holy fog along this narrow beach
where, despite a sunless sky,
cedar timbers bleach.
You're more optimist, John, than I.

A drunk staggers sideways in the swell,
spitting blood, muscatel, and crabbing,
cursing his sunken hull. His arctic breath
is icy on my cheek and in those native eyes
an ancient pain, like fog,
curls long and wide and dull.

Natural History

Late afternoon, autumn equinox,
and my daughter and I
are at the table, silently eating
fried eggs and muffins,
sharp cheese and yesterday's rice
warmed over.

We put our paper plates
in the woodstove and go outside:
sunlight fills the alders with
the geometries of long blonde hair,
and twin ravens ride roller coasters
of warm September air
out, toward Protection Island.

Together we enter the roughed-in room
beside our cabin and begin our chores together:
she, cutting and stapling insulation
while I cut and nail tight rows of cedar.

We work in a silence broken only
by occasional banter. I wipe the cobwebs
from nooks and sills, working on my knees
as if this prayer of labor could save me,
as though the itch of fiberglass and sawdust
were an answer to some old incessant question
I never dare remember.

When evening comes at last,
cooling arms and faces, we stop
and stand back to assess our work together.

And I remember the face of my father
as he climbed down a long wooden ladder
thirty years before. He was a tall strong sapling
smelling of tar and leather, his pate bald
and burnt to umber by a sun
blistering the desert.

He strode those rows of coops
with a red cocker spaniel and tousled boy-child
at his heel. I turn to look
at my daughter: her mop of blonde curls
catches the last trembling light of day.
Weary, her lean body sways.

Try as I might, I cannot remember
the wisdom of fourteen years, those pleasures
of discovery. Eron smiles. We wash up
at the woodstove as the sun dies into
a candle-flame. A light breeze rustles the first yellow leaves
of autumn as boughs slowly darken.
A squirrel, enraged, castigates the dog
for some inscrutable intrusion,
and Eron climbs the ladder to her loft.

Suddenly, I am utterly alone,
a child gazing up at his father, a father
smiling down on his daughter.
A strange shudder comes over me
like a chill. Is this what there is
to remember: long days roofing coops,
the building of rooms on a cabin, the in-
significant meal?

Shadows of moments mean everything
and nothing, the dying landscapes
of remembered human faces frozen
in a moment. My room
was in the basement, was knotty pine,
back there in diamondback country.

The night swings out over the cold Pacific.
I pour a cup of coffee, heavy in my bones.
Soon, this fine young woman
will stare into the eyes of her own son or daughter,
years blown suddenly behind her.

Will she remember only this ache,
the immense satisfaction of this longing?
May she be happy, filled with the essential,
working in twilight, on her knees,
with her children, at autumn equinox,
gathering the stories of silence together,
preparing to greet the winter.

Kah Tai Purgatorio

I could carry a little boat out
through sandy hillocks and marsh grass

and slip it into the water and slide
over that blue-green glass in silence.

I could cruise the waterways of winds
around this small lagoon where
terns nestle into shadows and herons wade.
I could, I could.

I want, like this little body of water,
to let my body reflect the stars and moons
of midnight. I want to lie that still.
I've seen this water calm as a dreamy boy.

But then I'd have to, sooner or later,
return. And doing so, I'd have to choose.
And any bank I chose
would be the world.

Requiem
For Kenneth Rexroth

1.

All day I wandered the difficult reverie of the sea
and the sea sang back to me that old song
of summer, "To Love is to Live," and the sun settled
lightly on the water. The interstellar silence between rainfall
and rainfall is all
that we need know of love, and all that we may learn of life
is that to die need not mean death.

The old hull slowly disintegrates among the stones
of its last long resting place and bears a silence
heavy like a shadow; the iron railings flaking
off into rust, the old battered timbers nourishing salt air
and sea mist. But there was a time

she creaked with delight and bore tuna in her hold, and strong
young men worked her shifting decks.

Now that the nets are gone, brass fittings stripped
from the wheelhouse, cobwebbed and dank, now that the anchor
is dragged away? The tedious afternoons pass us by
unnoticed, the epics of our days. These tides
do not respect our work. And yet, to work
is the meaning of the tides and they steadily eat away
the memories of old labors we abandon.

Because it is summer and the sea is beautiful, we think it
enough just to be here, walking, sighing
to the sighs of the sea. There were others
who walked this beach to sing
a little song of charity and death. They still sing, but far beyond
our ears. Few are they who hold in mind our prehistoric life.
Fewer still learn to bow to what they cannot have.

Even in dry summer, the sea winds sing our praise. But we
think it a cold song, shudder, complain, and turn away.
Farther from home than we ever dreamed we could be,
the days break over us like dreams these rains
can't wash away. If *to live* means *to love*,
to work gives form to what we say: each day
we struggle to make the day.

There was a man, now gone, who sang this song to me.
I didn't believe it then. He begged a price
I didn't know how to pay. But now that he is gone,
dead, as they say, I place my trust in him, in eighty years
of faith, his long life's love that settles down
like rain upon the sea, lightly down on everything,
like breath settles lightly into air.

2.
Suppose one human voice must speak,
suppose one human sound must stretch

across numberless gray casts of evening, in chill
of hoarfrost before the puffs of hope
chimneys breathe against despair—then let
that voice be calming, a warming sound that bends
against the air curving back
across the breath it comes from, that no one hear
without the deliberate act of listening: our time
is near. The animal-like phrases
we attempt to trap in voices
move beyond our eyes, shadows
melting into shadows
we never learned to read.

When a man ascends the stage of his own imagining,
he delivers there the grand summation
of his suffering, his one long
accounting of his days which disappeared
more quickly than his faith. His song
is plain. His music,
lowly, like his shame. The stillness in the air
at eventide, the stillness in the leaves at that
singular moment before they ride
the last ride down to earth, the still perfectly still
body of the hunter with his finger on the trigger,
squeezing lightly between the hammers of his heart:
these motionless moments
we only glimpse in passing.

After love, after the soft white cry of love
is stoppered in the throat, these little revolutions
of the soul are caught between breath
and breath, between the blood
and the body in its tremors. Who then
will remember the ambiguity of desire, duplicity
hidden in the semi-public kiss? Per-
functory and self-serving. Wavering . . .
hesitant . . . faulty . . . no wonder

we strangle on our doubts. Raccoons that haunt these shores
blend into the dusk. Can we
do less? We see them
walk on tiny hands to steal scraps we leave.

It is only when we must move, similarly simply,
toward that secret something
basic as our breathing that we
can learn to trust. What troubles us
most deeply is ourselves—a voice that longs to make
itself into a fist or a hand
to touch. We want to slow our pace
to match the little steps of animals who feed at night.
If we must blend into the blending grays
of dusk, then we must learn
to wait, watching from the corners of our eyes
until the remembered glimpse of warming fires
blazes up again
a long way down the coast around the bend
where evening fog comes toward us hushed and slowly
like a friend.

3.
Out the long road with its ruts and cracks
and tire-battering patches, past fields
of spotted cows and fat summer horses, past
the last few stands of woods, past new houses
with indoor plumbing and interest rates,
out,
past the end of the city water line and up
the hill beyond the old shake mill into
a world of promise,

and then the dirt country road
lined with alder and evergreen, broadleaf
fern, rhododendron, camas
and chamomile, and up

the narrow drive
where branches batter my battered truck,

I wheeze
to a stop. This brief northwestern summer allows
a little dust
to remind me
of all those summers back

in that country I'll never shake
from my boots: red dust
and prickly heat. Now scraggle of underbrush
almost too thick to walk through,
but I walk out,
climbing through it, smelling it,
watching for juncos and swallows and thrushes,
boots growing damp from night-mist,
senses
confused with memory: Wasatch,
Rockies, Tetons, Sangre de Cristos, Brooks Range,
Chugach, and now, suddenly,

the Olympics, ten years ago, immensely blue
in the distance. And I know
the rain never stops in Ketchikan,
the rain never came
to Utah, . . .

all those countries now
one country in
my mind . . .
so different, so lonely
that poetry can't reach it. Nor can I.

But I wade through it, tangle
and bramble, I wade and plunge

through rotting broken limbs and twigs toward
bluffs rising over the Sound where winds
grow thick with salt-smells
and islands in the distance
rise, rise and fall
in swells: San Juans, Queen Charlottes
of Canada; and beyond them, across the long
Pacific Rim, Japan
and northern China. I would speak across
years. T'ao Ch'ien, do you hear?

And why is it
I must come out here alone? Never with
a friend. For a man, for a man
in the middle of his years, there is a need
without name, an old memory or promise
broken: my mother, almost eighty now, but years
and years ago, my mother, her eyes a river of tears
for something I'd said
for no reason.

Gull-cries.
Cormorant scuds.
Clouds and clouds and clouds.
My father four years dead
and buried in that half-imagined land. He died
holding his woman's hand. I learn to live
alone
in a house I slowly build, and know
my own daughter will likewise
wound me. My brown Persephone so far away,
listen to this sea.

It churns, it breaks against these black
basaltic bluffs, and in the blue
swirls and curls of water, tentacles
of kelp beds absently waver.

Suppose I cried out against
the immensity of these blues—*ocean, sky,*
or *mountain*? Would anyone hear
or care? I wouldn't give a damn.
When the sun begins its fall, it makes me
sickly dizzy—birds, suns, sea-wrack. I'd paint
these mountains black. Little wonder
old Jeffers grew so vile: he knew
what we feel inside.

Thirty years ago, I used to lie
on my back in the haystack to listen to the stars.
Dusk then
was a kind of silence I haven't heard since, the unutterable
gray dying light across a range of gutted mountains
smoky-black with greed.

Lie quiet.
Listen. Is that
the first nighthawk
searching yellow evening light? The sound
of evening appetites:
peee-ik, peee-ik, peee-ik.

Turning to the trail back home, there is
so much vanishing behind us, so very much
to come, and all that ravaged country
spread out beyond all comprehension,
beyond imagination.
Pray that it will heal.

Coming across me here, along these old logging trails,
along game trails leading us back from the sea,
do you think me a gentle man, but sad?—not unlike
that man you knew once as a child,
who wagered with the sun

and lost,
who made you lovely promises—so long ago
that you can't quite remember,

although you remembered for a time.
This sea, you think,
smells like the great salt wastelands of
the West. The same gulls break and cry. The same hearts
break, night after night,
when the same voices
steal into our sleep.

Kochininako, Yellow Woman,
take my hand.
This silence that steals into my speech is there because
there are so many promises
I've tried and tried to keep.

4.
Is it still there, Canyon de Chelly,
high walls streaked
the color of new blood or of fire?

Once—a long time ago, it is true—but once
I went there alone, looking
for god-knows-what, and found
what the Greeks called *Eikos*, a holy place,

evening sunlight orange,
fiery as all history, and I walked for a time
in no particular direction, lost
to all purpose, but
learning,
slowly learning: apple trees, pear trees,
a spotted pony in a narrow corral.

I was a child of no country
but the country of the heart. I felt
the hands of the dead slide up
beneath my shirt. And now when I write or speak,
there is dying on my hands, dying
to flavor my speech.

I tried to sleep. A quarter moon
slipped over the canyon rim to filter
through the trees. The flanks of the canyon
were fleshy in a light
as after twilight
when I rose from a brown saddle blanket
to walk among the ghosts: my body
moved as though it belonged
to another, an ancient melancholy
dragging me down into the past.

But every canyon, like every street,
is a doorway, and we are beggars
knocking softly for entry. The busy people
pass us in silence, their eyes focused carefully
an inch beyond our heads or
just beyond our feet. For fear,
they look away.
Our secret whispered entreaties
are fruitless, falling
like dry grass through summer drought,
and we turn again
toward night and the thirst of heat.

Did I sleep? I remembered the body
of a woman I loved once, who
wouldn't speak, how, with her child
nursing, her breasts dried up, and nothing, she said,
would ever be the same. Her furtive eyes
glistened in the dark like little fires

burning on a hill. I held her face
for nothing in my hands until
I thought it would break.

Sweet, delicious smell of rain.

So many years since the hoeing. It is too easy
saying, Here is Ira Hayes
dying in a ditch. My people were not heroes,
but died there, too. No one mourned
except when the crop was good.

The waters and the beggars
come and go, the cruel light of years
claws our eyes. Are there still
memories in the ashes
rains wash slowly from the canyon? The memory
of women weaving baskets
from a time before they were meant for tourists? Is anguish
the only sound of water? Or is it
longing. And what would it mean
if we could walk again together
through ruins years have left behind, our hands
together,
eyes steady on each other's eyes? Would
the same crickets sing down there along the river
if we paused for love on the bank?

I who inhabit
the River-with-one-bank
have been too long with the sea, too long
with the slow rub of fog
and all those old songs
of the dying.

Now when light rain comes calling,
when it kisses the edge of my sleep, I dream

of scarlet ocotillo flowers
blooming after rain, so long
in the waiting, in the desert, waiting,
their blossoms so suddenly, *ocotl*,
torches, burning after rain. Whether their burning
is the burning of cities, the remembrance of Canyon de Chelly
when armies passed in the night to torch
houses, fields, and orchards,
when the dogs and children died—

or whether it might be
my own heart, our hearts,
inflamed
by some spark without reason—
that old hope and joy—
I cannot say.

5.
The dead of summer and nothing moves,
not the sky of weathered slate
nor the faces of strangers
pasted in their rooms above the street,
expressionless or strained. The joyous intervals
that pass us by remain mute, committed now
to memory's coldest cells. *Once,*
the poet sang, *once only.*

And then no more?
The murky tide that washed our feet
draws slowly back to sea.
The young couple in the doorway
linger to embrace.
This, and then the earth?

Yesterday was berries on the beach.
I dozed beside a fire and heard

or dreamed foghorns on a summer afternoon
like sirens enticing us
toward reefs hidden by the waves.
I woke, chilly and afraid.

This dead weight we carry
like an ancient grief is ours
because we will it—the lonely burden
of the verb *to be* as it becomes attached
to *living* or *alive,* day by day. So it's not to say
we can't, or won't, go on.
But on this earth, in
the middle of our trespass, we are
invisible, we are only shadows
sliding into night, pausing to give names
to the things that shape our passing: *saguaro,*
thimble-berry, madrone. Or *charity.*
Or *love.* Tell me it isn't fruitless, this moment
in which John Coltrane breaks my heart
from a phonograph, or that moment
long ago when I was lost in Beethoven's
great pastoral as the wind
swept away the desert endlessly.

As long as the tongue can open to the vowel,
as long as we can rise into
each day, just once, rise, and rising,
move the hand
to *act,* it remains for us to praise:
the fine red dust of Escalante,
light rain or mist of summer on the coast,
almond groves of the northern San Joaquin,
the clarity of temple bells, Kyoto after rain.

Could I feel the fingers that brushed my lips
just once,

so very long ago, then
I could praise.

Goodbye, we say, meaning
happy passing,
or *kind beyond.* But we
are only shadows
pausing as we pass high over the earth to say
our little praise. The old madrone
that trembles in the wind
can't help us, the absolute calm of animal eyes at night
cannot be our calm.

But once, once
leaning in a door
that opens the other world,
we pass our moment,
and suddenly know the earth
that we were a part of, once.

George Seferis in Sonora

It is most true that eyes are form'd to serve The inward light, . . .

—Sydney, "Astrophel and Stella"

No, I can't touch these mountains.
I have no word for the long shadows of saguaros
lengthened by the full moon of April. I've seen
how you wrap these mountains in highways, how
the natural numbers of Sonora accumulate
until you suddenly realize
they always total zero. At 4 A.M.
when the traffic dies and the moon embraces the Pacific,
I'm up
and drinking coffee, my nose in George Seferis.

Whatever you told me, I had to learn it by ear,
I had to memorize the touch—I couldn't believe my eyes.

How else to account for fingers that touched me once
and then vanished: of course they were roses
dying of the sun, they were songs doves sang
to begin another morning. It's always that
exactly: the untouchable other world
that touches us most deeply. Paris lay down
with a shadow, he lay down with an empty tunic,
and thousands died, but they did not die
for Helen. It was no goddess or mortal
they died for: not Helen, but the idea of Helen betrayed them.
And surely this desert is a woman who knows

God first invented blood
and then the thirst for blood, that each man is a Paris
who returns, anonymous, clutching an empty tunic.
To speak of the desert, I must return
to the Ancients, to the memory of some unspeakable failure.

Even to speak of Troy
in this city in Sonora, even to dream of Troy—
it is brutal. So I rise, old somnophobiac, before the day begins,
to write in the blood of our race, to save
what cannot possibly be saved,
and now, the first songbirds long before dawn, mockingbirds,
add their *gloriae, gloriae,* to the morning.

•

Sometimes the dove, that old cliché,
is more a moan than a song
when it sings *woe, woe,* and huddles on its limb.
A veil of fragile clouds
marbles the eastern sky. In Alexandria, they say,

it's the nightingale who wounds us. Here, we listen
to the terrible silence of the past, the enormous cost
of our decision to forget. Yesterday, as you trimmed
a dying bougainvillea, you pointed
across the way to another, entirely in blossom.
"They like the sun," you said, "and this one
gets very little." Oh, it was the color of blood,
it was beautiful all right.

And I wanted to give you a flower, but the garden
was all weeds, there were no roses, no asphodels
for me to bring to ease our mutual regret,
only these few coarse words
an old man sings in a broken voice when he's humbled
by a desert. There's a desert
each of us endures. It's beautiful there,
and deadly: whatever we give away
comes back to us, it's true, so I bring you
the whole of the moon as it passes, the fallen
petals of roses crushed into a powder,

this sort-of-a-song
rattling my heart with its singing.

But it's not about a desert. No,
I can't reach your mountains, I have no word
for these highways wrapping a heart for storage.
When the moon returns
bulging with its promises and warnings,
I will have no word to name them. The roads
that lead back from Sonora as though from the ancient temple
are a song a choir sings
in a long-forgotten language, the long body of our dreaming,
a lattice-work for rose-vines blooming by inward light
our eyes were made for seeing. And now,

in the harsh first light of day,
mockingbirds sing *gloriae, gloriae absurdus.*

Hellenic Triptych

Forehead on forearm, eyes unfocused,
he listens to rain pelting wet earth that smells
of dreams and destinations, of departures which
preceded no arrival. Alone with the long afternoon,
he longed for starlight through windows,
for the soft, hollow breath of the sea as it sounds
through the broken conch of the human voice
traveling its distance alone.

There was a time he thought of his body
as a temple for Helen, a time when the twin fires of his tongue
were his daughters, Justice and Mercy, but
that is the way of the young. Helen,
kidnapped by Theseus much as our bodies are taken:
for the moment—before the life escapes into Hades—
and we waken to dawn confused, everything forgotten,
everything but Helen.

And so he sets sail from Troy, forehead
bent to forearm, the afternoon slipping by
with its cargo of dream and remembrance.
So that is how the summer died.

•

At dawn, he'd taken
a solitary step and entered
the nearly perfect syntax of the world.

It would be simple to die for a Helen.
It would be easy to set sail, to turn one's back on the ruins,
to acquire the grammar of wisdom
at the small cost
of some small life:
to perfect a civilization.

Arrival is not destination, nor death
a suitable answer.

Each step the first step; each step the final:
each road a crossroad: each tree
articulates tree.—It is that which comes closest
but passes, that suggestion of perfection,
that makes the flesh its home.

⦁

And now, he knows, the evening comes
with its torment and its thugs
demanding taxes. And then the anonymous night
with its quicklime of desire,
its starlight and retribution.

That is how this window came to look out
on grief, on the charred monuments of Troy:
it would be good to give one's life for the beautiful
if the beautiful would last. But the world
casts us out and it is impossible to touch anything
except one another. So we reach out when we can

for the outstretched hand of another,
knowing that when it is withdrawn . . .

Head tilted forward
almost as though to pray, he buries

his eyes in his forearm.
And the gesture
is almost perfect.

A Word for Spring

We've returned; we always set out to return
to solitude, a fistful of earth, to the empty hands.
                                                    —George Seferis

Once more we step
from the cold solitudes of winter
into the solitudes of spring. Once more,
yellow daffodils and lilies
are the cruelest month.
I used to love to walk down Water Street
where crates of oranges and bananas
and heads of cabbage and lettuce were
stacked shoulder high. I used
to watch the unknown people pass
beside the miracle of the sea
talking to each other
as though the sea were a thousand miles
away and didn't know the secrets of our blood.

Sometimes, I think the sea is
listening to our lies; sometimes,
I think it hears us groping in the dusk.
If it does, it remains at ease
despite us. If we could understand
the rhythms of the tides, if we
could reach into the shadows of the bay,
we too could sleep through the long
and lengthening sunshine of the day.

We pause between the coffee and the cigarette,
between the talk that wakes us and the sleep
of solitude that punctuates our speech,
studying our hands like exiles
bent above a map that set us on our way.

The secret meeting place
where water and land join hands
could be our place. Were it not
for the red and the white of our veins,
our hearts would pump
pure sea water to our minds and lungs
and we would learn to breathe
according to the moon. But we
are lonelier than that. Someday soon,
the old days will come back. I loved
the bread I broke between my hands,
the taste of wine from someone's lips,
the emptiness of Water Street at night when spring
was ripe and everything was mine.

Reading Seferis
To Olga Broumas

"Not many moonlit nights
have given me pleasure."
The stars spell out
the ancient mathematics
of the heart in huge
desolate zeros, ciphers
of nothing, and despite it all,
I care. There is a fatigue
in the crumbling of cities
for which there is no cure,

no penance or catharsis,
not even a prayer—only
the will to endure. The heavy
torpor of gray-brown air,
the lethargy of the soul—
by these we measure out
each crisis, each ancient debt
we don't repay the poor.

There are not many moons
I remember. The Sound
is blue where it reflects
the dark sky of night
or the bright sky of day.
Amica silentia lunae,
and each day the sun
drowns in fire and water,
a metaphor for nothing,
our unaccountable longing.
Some would call upon the moon
for power, for pure sexual
pleasure, but that is unholy
and denies both the sowing
and the reaping. The moon
is not a scythe that mows
the tall mute grass of heaven.

But we, Olga, are grasses
wavering in breezes
of politics and dollars, we
are the exiles of the earth,
the rooted and swarthy who see
the moon in everything
and think it a symbol
for our suffering. It is
the human mind that curves
into a razor, that harvests

human pain. We shall be
the chaff which flies
in the cutting, the lullaby
of fields that is not heard
on moonless nights because
only moonlight is romantic.

I hear the lullaby of victims
who are happy. Few are the moons
for them, and even these
are imagined. I imagine the
full moon of a smile, the moon
of my buttocks when I was a boy
and a prankster, the twin
moons of my lover's breasts,
the stars, oh, in her eyes
and I love her. Olga, these
are the maps, topographies
of the heart that tell us
everything: we are all
the victims; we are heroes
also, and slaves. Seferis says
heroes are the ones
move forward in the dark.

I remember the terrible
darkness of my childhood
and the fear. And the moon
was more fearsome, more awe-full
with its wails and howls
and its shadows. I remember
the moon as female, Loba, yesterday
when she raged. I tire so soon
of metaphor! I want to send you,
Olga, this alphabet of stars
which ask for nothing
and offer a little light

against the dark we wear;
I want to offer the warmth
of a lullaby, the kiss
of deep sleep, a reflection of the moon
reflected on the waters
of your song—so few

are the moonlit nights
that I've cared for.

Old Bones

1.
All the quiet afternoon splitting wood,
thinking about books, I remembered

Snyder making a handle for an ax
as he remembered Ezra Pound

thirty years before,
thinking about Lu Chi.

Using the ax, I forget the ax.
Closing my eyes, I see.

2.
Thirty-one new yellow daffodils
bloom in the little garden.

Alder seed covers everything
with little flakes of rust.

A breeze through evergreens.
Distant bird-trills.

When Hui Neng tore up the sutras,
his bones were already dust.

3.
Wanting one good organic line,
I wrote a thousand sonnets.

Wanting a little peace,
I folded a thousand cranes.

Every discipline a new evasion,
every crane a dodge:

Bashō didn't know a thing about water
until he heard that frog.

Black Marsh Eclogue

Although it is midsummer, the great blue heron
holds darkest winter in his hunched shoulders,
the blue-turning-gray clouds
rising over him like a storm from the Pacific.

He stands in the black marsh
more monument than bird, a wizened prophet
returned from a vanished mythology.
He watches the hearts of things

and does not move or speak. But when
at last he flies, his great wings
cover the darkening sky, and slowly,
as though praying, he lifts, almost motionless,

as he pushes the world away.

A Dragon in the Clouds

It is solstice—
hot, dry,
air too heavy to move,
mountains hazy blue.

I have been baking in the sun
with Euripides' fable of Helen.

And now, quietly,
a finch has flown down from the cedar
to perch on the windowsill.

And I realize
she is curious,
she is watching,

and has cautiously stepped closer.

The beauty of the tragic,
the tragedy of the lovely,

she doesn't know or care to remember.

She knows two things:
the world is flat,
and that she lives
on this side

of the only river
she cannot fly across.

She looks at emeralds
in the grass and sees
only common seed.

And now she has come closer
once again, head cocked,
surveying my naked body.

Her eyes are large
and wearied by their knowledge,

like Kawabata's eyes
which knew
only sadness and beauty.

I close my book very slowly,
lay my head on my arms,
and look her in the eye:

she has become my lover
and my dharma master.

Morris Graves says birds
inhabit a world without karma.

The Gift of Tongues

Everything I steal, I give away.
Once, in pines almost as tall as these,
same crescent moon sliding gently by,
I sat curled on my knees, smoking with a friend,
sipping tea, swapping coyote tales and lies.

He said something to me
about words, that each is a name,
and that every name is God's. I who have
no god sat in the vast emptiness silent
as I could be. *A way that can be named*

is not the way. Each word reflects
the Spirit which can't be named. Each word
a gift, its value in exact proportion
to the spirit in which it is given.
Thus spoken, these words I give

by way of Lao Tzu's old Chinese, stolen
by a humble thief twenty-five centuries later.
The Word is only evidence of the real:
in the Hopi tongue, there is no whale;
and in American English, no Fourth World.

"True Illumination Is Habitude"

A perfect half-moon glistens
in the mist high over
the young bamboo.

The smoke-stained glass
I watch it through
makes a perfect halo

around it, as though
the moon were full. Below,
the trees are doubly dark

where no breeze lifts
a leaf—nothing moves
that doesn't move

toward sleep. You move,
in another room,
into the Dreamtime world,

your hair flooding out
in soft waves
around your face.

The night is so
perfectly still
I can hear your every breath

above my beating heart.
The fire's long since
gone out.

Alone by my lamp,
I read Rexroth's
Signature of All Things,

and once again,
like that swift bird
rising from its ashes,

the old ghost rises
from the wreckage of
this world

to touch my semi-
conscious life.
Poetry, Tu Fu says,

that will last
a thousand generations
comes only as

an unappreciated life
is passed.
I lay aside the book

and rub my weary eyes
just as Po Chu-i did
reading Yuan Chen

on his boat, by candlelight
a thousand years ago.
I sit motionless

in the motionless night
while mist
deepens

and the whole house
cools,
and I listen to your breath

and measure it against
this slow, insistent tolling
of our flesh.

Historical Romance

1. *Alis Ubbo*

Hard rain pummels the *Avenida da Liberdade*.
The *Rio Tejo* is swollen
dark with silt and new hillside soil.
This same rain fell on the Phoenicians
who called this
"Delightful Little Port"
so many hundreds of years ago.

Even the beggars in the *Praca do Rossio*
have clothed their twisted limbs
and gone wherever beggars go.

We walk beside the Fountain of Maximilian,
rounding the square,
three of us arm in arm,
unaware that by morning
the Algarve would be closed,
the Costa Verde
a veritable island,
all bridges north and south
swept away downstream or out into the Atlantic.

Perched on its topmost hill
and growing darker by the hour,
the old gray stone Alfama,
eight stony centuries of blood
blackening its towers. We climb
the high walls and walk
its perimeter together,
pausing to search the city
from dank parapets at its corners.

Nothing but poor, black-shawled women
hanging out their laundry in the alleyways
of tenements,
nothing but a few old men with canes
and memories of war,
nothing but a few dirty children
throwing stones at alleycats or running through the rain.
Nothing changed in eight hundred years
but the bare-bulb glow of shabby rooms
one afternoon in autumn.

The same bread soup bubbles on a stove.
The same streets reek of fish and urine.
The same gray light stains everything it touches,
rich and poor alike.

A few swallows sail in the rain
over black slate roofs
as they did over Moors and Romans.
Barges and boats float slowly
down the huge brown river, round the bend,
and vanish.

We who have traveled across centuries
from a world we think is new
think this poverty is nostalgia,
that we don't belong to it.

My daughter speaks to them by name
and tells them about Brazil.
Because it is far away,
they think it must be better.

And we go back through evening light
and heavy rain,
back to our hotel to drink alone in the bar.
My daughter takes my face in her hands
and holds it like a mother:
Don't worry,
she says,
tomorrow we'll take the train
to Evora—
it's the only line that's left.

And my partner says,
And if that's not enough,
we can ride the bus all day—
those hard-backed seats—
and take in a *juerga* in Seville,
we can visit the Moorish gardens in the Alcazar
and search the bookstalls Saturday
for Spanish editions of Lorca and Alberti.

And if it's literary history you crave,
we'll take a single yellow rose
to throw into the river
for all the Spanish poets
who haven't any graves.

2. *Capela dos Ossos, Evora*

Laborare est orare.
Saint Francis, forgive them.
How can they know what they do?
—Pillars of skulls,
walls of human bones,
and in your name, they pray.

When I asked the old priest I'd spoken with on the street
how this chapel came to be built,
he pretended he didn't speak English;
and when my daughter asked
in pure, clear Portuguese,
he said he didn't know.

We stood inside a whole afternoon
in a silence heavy as syrup, the bones of the fearful
or of the unafraid
five hundred years locked in plaster,
five hundred years,
and the terror they promise
is eternal.

Outside the rain continued to fall.
Someone came in, knelt before the little altar,
and lit a single candle.
Being pantheist and pagan,
we knew it was time to go.

All night, hammer-blows of rain
rang the cobblestones.
Cold in the Spanish dark,
I screamed myself awake,
dreams of fire and bones and blood
shattering my sleep.

To the south and the west,
there are seas,
calm beaches, gentle evening breezes in the olive groves,

a history of so long ago it seems
almost a mercy, a pain so remote
we think we can embrace it,
naming it History, or Hellenism, or Love.

I cannot sleep.
"Labor *is* prayer,"
Tree repeats, and says a chapel built of bones
is a natural thing.
The temple, she says,
is neither in the bones nor of them:
they are the temple through which it sings.

3. *Plaza de Espana, Sevilla*

Riding all day on a cold bus through broken fields
and hills of wild flowers,
past relics of failed rancheros, there were birds we couldn't name
slumping down gray skies
above huge, black Andalusian bulls
standing aloof and dark,
watching nothing, like sullen, indifferent gods
about to embrace their wounds.

And then evening coming on and the first glimmer
of sunlight in a week,

rolling down from easy hills, city lights
soft in the east like sunrise,
the city before us like a postcard from the country
of a dream:
huge cathedral black against the sky,
its bell tower lit from below
like a masked face on Halloween
with a candle beneath the chin
to frighten all the children.

We eat gazpacho and chorizo and wander city streets
like any good *turista*. The Torre del Oro
rises dark and shining
from the banks of the Guadalquivir,
and everywhere, we think, we hear music:

and I want,
suddenly,
to learn the names of all the flowers in Spanish,
I want to visit
my ancestor's grave in Venice,
to bring him one defeated rose from Spain.

Turning back down narrow corridors leading toward our room,
our feet, unaccustomed to cobblestone,
ache and ache.
And something else,
inside,
cold and hard
like a stone inside the heart. But just before I fall asleep,
I think: Sevilla, . . . Sevilla, . . .
and call it softly, feeling with my mouth,—
Sevilla, . . . Sevilla, . . .
thinking it harsh and beautiful, beautiful and harsh
like love.

Dawn arrives with its wagonload of gold—
a clatter in the streets below,
and yellow sun so bright
even fine gauze curtains
can't protect my eyes.

The night's waves washed over me
and carried me out again into a dream:
a memory of music in the hills,
distant music and bawling sheep,
an old man with stubble on his chin
remembering the guns,
the black boots
of the Generalissimo
on the plaza forty-five years ago.

Walking in warm December sun
between two lovely women, why must I remember
only dreams of martyrs,
our unaccountable failures,
our national greed?

The great cathedral built on the wreckage of a mosque
tolls the morning hour:
nine o'clock.

By ten, we're in the plaza:
the river, still and blue,
curls slowly under bridges
along the colonnade.

We walk along
looking at coats-of-arms
remembering what we can

of the failed revolution
until we come
to the Capitania General:

two military guards with burp-guns
stand outside the hall.
The first steps forward
and waves us on our way.
His eyes are dead.

Beyond the river, in the Parque de Maria Luisa,
there are jasmine and rose-trees,
narrow lanes among fountains,
and a monument
to the poet Gustavo Adolfo Becquer,
complete
with Cupid and swooning girls—
the dream of a past before the past we see.

Soon, we will fly all night
in a drone above the Atlantic.
We will bring back everything we were given.

Who has heard the sound of boot-heels echo
on the flesh-colored tile of the plaza

will remember.
And remember roses in December
purchased from a pushcart in the plaza,

and the myrtle labyrinth
and infinite corridors
of the Alcazar.

It is autumn in a city we have dreamed.

The maple leaves are turning red, the night
grows long and cold.

We will fly west until we vanish in the sun.

It is beautiful and sad
the way we,
dying,

make monuments of the dead.

Seated Figure

It is a long way from there to here.
It is longer than all the old roads of exile,
longer even than the silence of the heron.
The landscapes changed. Someone
numbered the dead. Someone mapped the pain.

Once, they say, the animals came to us
and licked our palms for the salt,
and looked at us with huge, knowing eyes,
then turned and left
alone. And entered Paradise.

Dresden Cattle

Oh, the ruins of the human heart.
Like a barn gone up in flames,
like a bombed cathedral,

the shadows of almost human forms
fall or rise or slide
silently by, entering the dark

and light by turns—Napoleon
or the Slavs that died
along the dying Elbe.

The old blue marbled hands
of the mason set stone upon stone,
and the bloody hands of the bitter

made them shatter.
We were herded through the streets
like cattle. We cried

but no one came. It is one thing
to love another human being,
another to know

and remember
the way the beautiful died.

Blue Monody
Blues for Thomas McGrath

And now the winds return,
blowing in from the sea,
driving summer steadily away,
south toward tall palms
we dreamed of when we were children
shivering in snows
that never ended.

And now these winds return
with frozen hands and laughter,
tormenting mountains,
twisting trees until you think

that like any human heart
they cannot bend farther
and will surely break.

I've kept my heart in my hands
through all these storms and seasons.
I've held it tight.
When the great trees bend
and their groans are almost human,
I've looked up more than once
from the desk where I invent a life,
looked up stunned
when they cried out,
thinking it a friend
arrived for comfort in the cold,
or my own harsh voice
grown suddenly old and fearful,
the fitful cry of a man whose name
was never counted among the names
of the innocent
and now must face the winter.

I've held my heart
in my hands and pushed
my breath across it
to blow the snow away.

Traveling, traveling, I've learned
a few exotic names
and places where great deaths occurred,
where the lonely
are buried in their trenches,
in mass graves which couldn't,
under all that earth, disguise
the misery carved
into ordinary faces.

The winds continue to grieve
although the dead ask nothing
from us now. And nothing
is what we gave: I've held tight
to this heart I could not break
like an egg to eat.
The wounds, the wounds I bore
were not my own,
but this hunger is all mine.
These trees, defeated by the wind,
endure: they cling to the earth
and won't let go
despite sea-winds drumming blows.

●

Down in the bay, the old wharf
slowly crumbles,
gray wood bleached almost white,
huge timbers ruptured.
Homer thought a field of lovely asphodels
would mark the homelands
of the dead, but we know
differently, having seen
those faces rising from the sea
a thousand times or more,
their own chewed hearts
rotting in their hands, each
marching slowly inland
with his broken oar.

No matter how far inland
we may stray,
we can't escape the sea.
Each heart longs to be
Odysseus, to bear its wounds

forthrightly,
long enough not to survive,
but to embrace,
if only once again,
Penelope. Here
on a gnarled coast, winds play
cruel jokes, twisting trees
into almost human forms
reminding us of nothing
so much as our own brutality.

Cold September winds blow in from the stormy sea.
I've got my heart in my hands again.

If you pass by, do not think that I
am not afraid.
Winds will drive me down beneath the waves,
under ravaged trees I cannot save.
They are neither laurel nor myrtle;
nor am I
a Milton;
nor you
a Lycidas,
nor dead.

Here is the wreckage of a heart:
take it from my hands.
No one understands
the winds or the sea. We mourn because
we are alive. I give you this monody.

•

It is true, as the poet sang, Elder Brother:
 Every angel terrifies.
I've never seen an angel, but I've heard

those cries of a desperate cat,
bawling with and without her Tom,
the sexual need to scream
the soul's desire, the cries
we all come from . . .
every angel terrifies. Because
there is also
always a little ugliness inside,
every angel terrifies.

The deep sexual wail of the alley cat
is purest song:
uncluttered by metaphor or meaning,
it says nothing but what it is—
the single note of desire without cunning,
its only meaning *being,*
—we confuse the sound; we have our self-
deceptions to consider—we
who are burdened with enormous
intentions to remember.

Everyone is desperate,
singing solo.
Night comes down hard
and we turn alone in bed
toward bare needs we'd meant
to leave behind.
We listen to the dark
and hear only winds and waves
that never stop.
Somewhere
between nightmare and insomnia,

stars conspire to wink and shine.
Old Compañero, I tell you,
the thought of singing solo
terrifies.

Bird on the hill,
little cricket
itching in the grass, . . .

. . . bitterness like a razor on the tongue . . .

. . . it is hard, brother,
seeing those blank faces
of battered mothers
at the marketplace,

hard looking into
empty eyes
of children
who die
a little every night.

"The soul
to know itself
must look into a soul"—
and sing.
There is always
that old eternal
other side of things—
which brings us
to our knees.

A mirror is not a soul. It's not
for daily trivialities,
not even for our own
self-centered lone-
liness that we listen
at the heart of things.
Stoked on drugs
and driving at light-speed
down a dead-end street,
there's barely time to think.

What terrifies
most deeply
is what we see
inside: every angel
driven out by lies.

Jeezus-gawd-aw-mighty,
        there were angels in your eyes!

Imagine Hoover
waking alone in the night,
thinking hard on your fate
and on the fate of your sisters and brothers,
flat-nosed, square-jawed, no-neck bigotry
swirling him into vertigo,
nauseous,
choking on his own poison phlegm
("*Nigger!*" "*Kike!*")
as the faces
(black and white)
march past him:

his allies:
the Senator from Wisconsin,
Joseph McCarthy, and his cronies:
Bobby Kennedy and Richard Milhous Nixon;

and the House Committee
on Un-American
Activities

—a Commie in every bed,
a socialist in every bath—

and those who made the Blacklist,
not least of all
the proletarian angel, Tom McGrath.

Hoover sweats and clutches his heart
and tries to focus his eyes on his night-light.
The angels of dead civil rights
workers march slowly, inevitably by,
bloody, marching toward breaking daylight in the east.

Confluences, visitations,
demon ghosts of the present arrive here from the past.

The Ghost of Christmas Present?
There is no peace.

And every angel terrifies.

•

Is that it?
Carbuncles on the skin of the body
politic?

Ten years ago,
snug in his little house
on this high, wind-blistered bluff,
low fire
in the stove despite
it being mid-summer
in the Northwest,

Tom McGrath sank deep into his chair
and turned warm eyes
opaquely back on time
to remember thorny years
lost in the depths
of "hornacle mines"
winding labyrinths
deep beneath

the infected and infesting streets
of the City of Lost Angels

until, at last, he escaped
into the long bleak night of the frozen north,
leaving Marsh Street
(*Marsh* Street! In L.A.!) leaving Marsh Street
and the hornacle mines behind,
and entered the thirty-year Christmas
of his wild mid-American dream-dance
imagining a friend.

The Revolution lurched somewhere
out there among rubbish
left behind
by pale men
who manned the picket lines.

Times were thin.

He lit a cigarette from a cigarette,
rolled his eyes,
and grinned, "K-e-e-e-rist,
you haven't seen anything
until you've seen the winds
sweep Moorhead
after the snow has frozen!
I swear you can *see* the cold!
Gawd, I'd hate to grow old up there."

From hornacle mine to beet packing plant,
we followed, . . .
going down there over the river, . . .
alone,
over the river, . . .
over winter ice.
We were all lost together,

gloriously lost along the way,
searching for a heaven of blue stars,
building the Big Kachina,
demonic, believing in
loving Gaia,
loving believing,
being
being our only poem,
the truly revolutionary act,
poesis,
process
of becoming. . . .

And there it is
in the hexagrams
of yesterday's *I Ching;*
there it is,
written in piss in new winter snow beneath a cold blank sky
        a thousand miles from nowhere,

a few miles down the road,
over the frozen river,
over winter ice. . . .

To have power over Nature,
to have power over Bird and Forest,
over Sea and Mountain and Wild Beast,
to dream of power,
to cling to the dream of power in the hour
of greatest need:

to have stood silent
is to conspire, is to concede.

And now, a little south of here,
the white train rolls,
the white train regularly rolls.

"To be men, not destroyers,"
that was the task
Grampa set, learning from his own
broken heart:
"wrong from the start, that stupid
suburban prejudice."
All I asked was this:
stars caught in the bristling bare branches of trees
before the ice storm brought them down,
the earth frozen and black; the river,
buried in shadow, no longer dreaming the calm, indifferent sea,
a little ice along its edges;

it is time
to face front,
get back on the line.

Strands of fog erase this stretch of beach,
swirls of fog erase the sky above the Sound.

To be takers, yes, to be sure; but to be givers
also; to surrender
The Goods;
to be
searchers for the art
of the sublime
gift of courage to face front and get back on the line.

Carbuncles on the cold skin
of the Body Politic.

The thin black shadow of a Trident Nuclear Sub
dices the vast Pacific.

To be men,
not destroyers,
that's the trick.

Remember that night, just a few years ago,
we spent three hours sipping on a beer,
remembering Michael Harrington,
his body wracked with cancer,
his soft, patient voice
over Public Radio
offering every moral answer
to Reagan's lies and murders,
to George Bush's marching orders
against the Sandinistas,

and we toasted Norman Thomas,
you looking me in the eye
and asking how many will have to die
before the murders end,

and the juke box played a sad country song,
and you stood unsteadily, leaning on your cane,
and made a bad joke about Pound's posturing—
cane and cape and earring
during his early days in London
(the man wouldn't have been dumber
had he posed as Beau Brummel)—
and apologized for the music,
"but not for working class people—
rather have a beer in here
than anywhere else in the country."

Dirty floors and haggard faces,
dreams pissed away.

Neither disgraced nor enlightened,
these were the men in the trenches, the women
who sent their sons to war,
who worked the factories, who paid the taxes.

Everything's in order.
Some to die, some to be maimed, everything is ready.
Everything's been done.
We cross the avenue:
"Helluva life when crossing a gutter's
the biggest challenge of the day!"

(Safe at his desk, door cosily bolted,
stealing a moment, another, higher, poet
peers out his window: two floors below,
he sees the homeless go about their tasks,
and he records his heart to bursting,
he measures out his sympathies
before his lecture on form and epiphany—
probably at the expense of his graduate
seminar on Later Keats.)

The afternoon sun rides high above
the northern Mississippi. A few cars slide by
as we slowly walk
under maple saplings in fluttering leaves
along clipped lawns in an autumn breeze.

Across the street,
a man in greasy hand-me-downs
strides by with his sleeping roll.

"That one's been on the road
a while,"
Tom says, "probably tryin' to find a train."

And we are a long way
outside Yellowstone
and a longer way from Port Townsend.

The things we've seen will never come again,
and who'd want to live them over?
And nothing changes.

The poor are the same poor, and the dead and the dying
are the same.

Where is the meaning? "Six million dead"
mean nothing to us—we've only witnessed the photos—
our abstracted, two-dimensional, superficial understanding.
And the seven million Russians, Estonians, Latvians, Lithuanians,
figures reaching ever-farther beyond the ability of the mind to grasp?
Don't ask.

It is one thing to stand against murder,
and another to do without supper.
We stammer and cuss and blame one another.
The heavens continue to burn.

Somewhere in transit, somewhere driving toward
        Pah-Gatzin-Kay or Boston,
crossing the Great Mountain, say,
that lies just outside of Moorhead,
the sound of the sea comes back to us
like the voice of long dead sailors,
familiar with its longing,
the hush of Puget Sound
when winds ride bluffs that rise above Fort Worden
and rattle the twisted limbs of brittle old madrona,
white flowers scattered to the winds,
winds,
when they return again each fall,
driving summer steadily away,
when all the winds and rains return with icy fingers, . . .

Homer thought a field of lovely asphodels would mark
the homelands of the dead.

What survives in the heart,
what endures,
lies just beneath what is said
when what is said
is said
just so:
only thus do we know
our own temple, our own heaven,
our hell, our home.

Cisco Houston sang,
You don't believe I'm leavin'?
You can count the days I'm gone.

      •

Yellow alder leaves fall
where madrona blossoms,
small, delicate, had fallen.
The grass is tall and brown, and apples
beckon yearling deer
who come down from wooded bluffs
to gorge until they're drunk.
Autumn fog tumbles along the water.
A few boats, a few seagulls
like an amateur painting.

Sunlight slants away, turning yellow.

I've been sitting on the deck of the same bar on Water Street
      for hours,
ignoring my whiskey,
watching the changing dance of sunlight on the water
as the day passes,

and I remember how badly
I would have wanted the whole damned bottle only five years ago
just to numb the aching,
and the whiskey-colored sun,
and its clattering light on the water,
my own self-pity
and the cry of the loon and the whine of a gull
and the toot of the out-going ferry.

I hang slack-jawed, empty,
a growing numbness just behind the eyes
although I am stone sober,

. . . *sadness, melancholy,*
or any of those other insufficient names we give to grieving,
or any of those other insufficient names we give to living,

while the puffins go on with their diving
and mountains in the distance turn black and then silver,
sky growing pale
and growing wider.

A shadow grows over me and I shiver.

Poised at the edge of the sea
like a damaged bird,
I keep one eye on each horizon:
westward, the vast implacable ocean
stitched to the wide indifferent sky;
to the east, mountains, and, beyond the mountains,
mountains, and the great rolling plains
where winds of change blow through our lives
like snows across the Dakotas, a cold blank nothing.

From the four corners of exile, from the cracks and ravines
of the ruptured human heart,

from the sea and the shadows of mountains,
a few friendly shadows,
a few friendly faces come back again
to taunt us, to lure us back on the line:

T'ao Ch'ien alone in his cabin
far from the intrigues of the city,
trying to give up the wine,
committed to his plowing,
resting only at night to write poems
remembering his old home on South Mountain;
sad, wise Tu Fu in exile, alone at his brushwood gate,
waiting to share his wine;
Saigyō gazing alone at the moon,
writing poem after poem;
Bashō and Ryōkan
alone on Sunset Hill
watching the River of Heaven pour down across Sado,
island of exiles in the Sea of Japan.

And I return to Helen,
exiled in Alexandria
while Troy burned.

Rexroth, exiled in Montecito
after forty years in the city,
wrote his best poems, love songs and elegies and his own epitaph.
What more could you ask?—a lifetime learning to speak simply.

When fame kneeled at the feet
of Georgia O'Keeffe, she, saintly, remained silent,
closed her door
and went on painting flower and bone and blank
pale sky, eighty-nine pages on file at the FBI.

Van Gogh, who couldn't peddle a painting,
saw only the same starry sky which demanded he learn to speak

with his entire body—he too
listening with his eyes.

"Life goes on," we say. "That's life."
Down Port Townsend Bay,
the paper mill blows sulfur smoke in columns of soft white cloud
as the evening shift begins.

In town, it grows late.
The bric-a-brac shops and antique dealers,
the Rotary Club and Republican steering committee and Chamber of
        Commerce
and city offices close for the night again.
The day's decisions have been made
without the counsel of T'ao Ch'ien.
It's Friday night.
There's a football game.

        •

And now the winds return, late,
to torment trees,
blowing autumn in from the sea.
These trees,
defeated by the wind, endure.

Faces rise through the night
as through water,
each with its blessing or its warning
we've heard a thousand times before,
each with its gift of hope and terror
we can't refuse,
each with its questions and its knowledge,

and the voices of trees groan or shriek in almost human form.
Exiled from the Garden,

this is the garden we murder and survive,
listening to days and seasons, to inconstant tides
and our own reflexive lies, refusing
to open our eyes to the enormous tragedy
of waterline and riverbed and darkened sky:
we struggle
to re-invent the Garden with insecticides.

Pythagoras thought form reflected
the irrational numerology of Pure Mind.
The Pure Mind of Buddhism
declares this world
illusion.

It is late.
The world sleeps or rises
or goes about its way. The wind blows.
The sea sighs. Someone, once again,
at midnight,
opens the book of the heart.
Trees rattle and groan.

We are not in the dark.
We are not alone.

Getting It Wrong Again

Civilizations are as short-lived as
days of our lives . . .
> —Czeslaw Milosz

and slowly, in the middle, I close the book and lay aside
the unreal world.

Clouds continue to gather overhead, outside,
sliding in from the sea.

Nothing distinguishes them, one from the other,
but bulk or weight or the pathetic tint
gray sunlight lends their hair.

Thus the universal devours each particular, each life
reduced to its essential. What
can I know
is not a question.

Of course I wanted power, I wanted
the power to save not a civilization, but
one small petal from its flower.

For in its perfect hour, it was lovely.
But not a week. Not even one whole day—
the perfect product of ten thousand
thousand years—perfection—

before a cleansing rain.
Before the hand
protects the heart
with its tight fist again.

Scrutability

Tu Fu, old and ravaged by consumption,
bent over his mulberry paper and wrote
the characters "single" and "wild goose,"
his eyes weakened by the moonlight.

Because it was October in his life,
he refilled his cup with wine.
His joys were neither large nor many.
But they were precise.

Lifer

McNeil Island Correctional Center, I:86

Hunched over hard white bread
and plastic soup bowl filled with gruel,
he looked like a stork, a silly angel,
all neck and bony shoulder-wings
and awkward beak.

His head lifted, then fell
in a slow deliberate dance,
three, four times, doughy-skinned
in a gray room sickened by yellow light.
He kept his eyes shut tight.

Outside the prison dining hall,
a turnkey slammed and locked
the heavy iron gate. The old man placed
his palms together softly, raised
them to his stubbled chin,

crossed himself, and ate.

Two Pines

1. *Yung Chia Reconsidered*

A wind in the pines,
moonlight trembling on the stream
at deepest midnight
on the coldest evening:
what does it mean.

2. Hakutsu's Pine

A great pine stands alone
beside the old stone house.
Examined in detail:
like meeting ancient sages
face-to-face.

Mountains and Rivers without End

After making love, we are like
rivers come down from the mountain summits.

We are still, we are moving,
calm in the depths of danger—

two rivers entering the sea
slowly, as if nothing matters:

quietly, but with great power,
merging in deepening waters.

Ten Thousand Sutras
After Hakuin

The body is the body of the Buddha.
Like ice and water, the one is always in the other.

In the middle of the lake
we long for a drink of water.

Adrift in Samsara,
we dream of blissful Nirvana.

This body is the body of the Buddha,
this moment an eternity.

Saying *I love you*, the deed is done—
the name and the deed are one.

With you and without you,
the line runs straight:

your body is the body of the Buddha,
there is light beyond the gate.

This love I give to you
is the love that comes from Kannon.

Every breath a sutra.
Going or returning, it's the same.

Our bodies are the bodies of the Buddha,
our names are Kannon's name.

No word can adequately say it,
yet every word must praise it:

in silent meditation
destroying evil karma,

in silent meditation
inhabiting the dharma,

this body is the body of the Buddha,
your body is the body of the Buddha.

Open arms and eyes to Samsara
embraced by the thousand arms of Kannon!

In the perfect mind of vivikta-dharma,
the truth of solitude,

our body is a temple
not a refuge.

Praise our body,
even in Samsara,

our bodies are the body of the Buddha,
our bodies are the body of the Buddha.

Kannon

I adore you. I love you
completely. Nothing to ask in return.

Each act of affection a lesson:
I fail, but with each failure, learn.

Like studying
under Te-shan:

thirty blows if I can't answer;
thirty blows if I can.

Destination Zero

1.
Over low, rolling hills patch-worked by live oak
and post oak and maple
and stitched by broken highways,
daybreak comes early, eastern sky
streaked with oranges and yellows that stir
the dove into song, that waken the mockingbird

who shakes the dew from white-tipped wings
and glides out over the fields to learn
whatever mockingbirds learn.

And I, too, have journeyed out of long darkness,
have risen
bewildered in the dark before dawn
in strange rooms smelling of smokestacks
in cities I could not name,
cities trembling beside plaintive trains that rumble through
on their long journey into memory.
I've risen to pull on the garments of this life
like a mourning shroud
and walked out into first light
to test my own wet wings.
Is it dream or remembrance, this image
of myself behind the wheel on the arc
of a long gray highway
winding from nowhere to nowhere,
any hills at all floating by,
a few clouds carried up
on the wings of wandering hawks,
and a heartland farmhouse crumbling on a ridge
above the rocky dry riverbed,
field of stubble,
rusty fences and the sagging flatbed truck
someone used once long ago for baling hay,—

all my life driving into the dawn,
through the morning and down
long afternoons into corridors of stars,

driving past the freshly painted First Baptist Church,
and the First Church of God
with its sagging foundation,
past the new brick First
Presbyterian Church that must own

the best scenic property in Heaven,
and the dirt-poor First Unitarian
clapboard church, and
the tidy First Methodist.
I am driving through "God's country" again.

Banks and churches cherish firstness.
The Bodhisattva
will be last to enter Nirvana.
It is daybreak and February in north Texas.
Daybreak shocks, it is so wide.

A mockingbird cries
and nothing moves. A slip of smoke
from a chimney just beyond the hill.
Fine mist swirls and burns away.

All outward journeys run parallel
to the journey that leads in,
the self unfolding like petals on a rose,
opening one by one and falling
one by one
as we journey toward the center
that reveals only elemental emptiness within.

The arduous journey out of self is a journey toward the dawn.
So why, this late in life
and with a hundred years in these eyes,
must I travel with the weight of the dead again,
with relics from some other life
like a map I cannot read, destination zero,
the heritage of blood.

Orphaned in this world, I have
buried my dead
in God's country
again and again. Lastness

has been my way. Give me
an old man's eyes, give me
the silence of the dead.
Lastness is my way.

At John Hall's farm in Mulberry, Texas,
I walked out to the pond and paused
to pluck a long gray feather
from a great blue heron's carcass—
shot by some witless kid.
It held the blue of the sky and nightfall gray
and the sound of the sea in its form.
But it was only a dead heron
like so many others,
putrid, buzzing flies.

Walking back across the fields, I watched
a crowd of cardinals gather in a tree,
the mockingbird called again and
a ragged old coyote
zig-zagged into the wash below the hill,
warily, not to be hung by his heels
from a gate, the way they do
in God's country.

Little white-tailed mockingbird,
Saint Mimic in the cathedral
of Our Lady of Perpetual Longing,
little down-and-outer, God's dog,
tattered trickster, show me the way.
I'm journeying out again, don't ask me why,
soul spreading shabby feathers toward
both edges of the onrushing dawn,
embracing the breadth
of the endless sky.

2.
Snow falls lightly on my adopted mother's
casket poised above
the gaping hole of her grave.
Suddenly, the sun breaks through
late February clouds with blinding yellow light.

She loved this land, Uintah,
Wasatch and La Sal mountain ranges
under snow, the striations
found in Wingate sandstone
in the canyons near Moab
where she was born
nearly ninety years ago.

And now she is dead with the one man
she loved, dead with her love
as with her lies and denials.

My name was Arthur Brown
when she first lied to me—
for my own good, she always said—
driving me "home"
from the orphanage to see
my father and my dog, she said.

"But that's *not* my father and
that's *not* my dog," I cried,
angry little three-year-old terrified
of the dark and the switch that stung my legs,
their farm an alien land,
"and you can't keep me here."
And I tried to run away.

So the road would be my way,
destination zero,

for thirty years, until
I came into the rain.

Forty-odd years have gone in a dream.
And now she is dead.
And I don't quite understand
exactly how to mourn
or how to grieve
over the one who kept the secret
when I was beaten to a scream.
The sun warms my face.
I loved her best from a distance.

The old woman, as was her way,
calculated everything, even death,
planned everything down to my ex-
wife's fortune, and instructed,
"no service, no funeral."
Two cemetery workers, one still
in the high seat of his backhoe,
and the driver of the hearse
who brought her body here,
patiently wait.

Her casket swings
almost imperceptibly
in a faint breeze,
ready to be lowered.

I raise one hand to signal
and the backhoe clangs
and nestles her casket into its gray
concrete sarcophagus, that final resting place.

The workers draw back again.
My daughter steps up alone and drops
a hothouse lily into the grave. I step up

and drop a rose with a single sprig of fern.
What my ex contributes
is between herself and the dead.
High clouds burn away.

A fierce heart demanded,
"No funeral. No service."
She would not cave in
to a Mormon god, would not indulge
the superstitions of her kin.

Sunshine turns to rain, rain to snow,
and snow gives way to sunshine,
all in a moment's time.

I step forward again
and present my mudra—*gasshō*—
and, whether or not she might approve,
recite the *Nembutsu,*
and bow again, *gasshō,*
and clap my hands just once: good-bye—

good-by to the willow switch that scarred my legs
in a life I scarcely remember;
good-by to deceits and denials;
good-by to all I refuse to forget
and to all she would not hear or speak; good-by
to the grief she willed
and to all the episodes she revised.

In her deathbed, her skin
was tissue-paper thin,
blue veins like rivulets beneath,
feet cold as February winds.
Her last breaths came
in measured, convulsive gasps
with a terrible silence between.

And then they stopped.
And that was the end.
I went to stand in the miserable cold
outside the hospital doors
and smoked a cigarette
while they bathed her and dressed her
and brushed her wispy hair into a wave.
Perhaps I wept.

And now she's laid to rest in frozen ground.
Good-by. I carry the name
of her betrothed, Sam,
but my name is also
Arthur Brown.
She knew it through forty years of lies.

And this prayer or song or summing up
is only the rattle of bones in an orphan's ear,
a talking-to-myself
to ease my fear
as bleak night descends.

And now I turn homeward again,
toward the soft drone of the rain, alone
again at last,
in winter light that is gun-metal gray and puts
a chilly ache in my bones.

3.
My old dog is dying.
For a year and more,
I've carried him like a rag
up and down the stairs
as he grew increasingly immobile.
And now he is dying
with all his undying devotion.

When asked, Do dogs
have Buddha nature?
he answered, "Arf!"

who now is dumb,
all rag and jutting bone and thinning hair,
his half-blue eye
almost blind.

When he falls,
he cannot rise.

I have carried him out of the house and onto the lawn
to bask in summer sun,
but his head falls sideways as he staggers,
collapsing in my lap
and slipping into a coma.

In an hour, he is gone,
head lolled over my leg,
eyes vacant, fierce
loyal heart finally stilled.

I scatter his ashes in the woods
beyond this house where we spent sixteen years.

It is late summer and rain, and spiders
spin their silver nets
among bamboo leaves,
and moss in the garden breaks into tiny white blossoms.

Evening after evening, I sit outside
alone, last hours slipping by,
lost in dying light,

listening to robins sing,
Twee-dee, tweedly-dee,
or watching trees grow
or the sky change shape,
destination zero.

So that is what I am.
Twee-dee, tweedly-dee.
Whatever the winds forgive,
they forgive with a sigh tonight.
Twee-dee, tweedly-dee.
And somehow, that's all right.

4.
These narrow highways plunge
through tiny mining towns
vanishing under Colorado mountains.
They draw a thread
across impossible deserts
or split the rolling hills of Iowa farms
no one will remember
except for a moment's regret.

Burying our dead, we write our lives
in disappearing ink, the landscape sliding by
just outside the window, the lost lake
of childhood followed hard
by the granite cliffs of divorce, and before
you know it, there's nothing left
but photographs
slightly out of focus, a vague visual note
about tamaracks painting valleys
somewhere west of Missoula
in what-the-hell-year-was-that,
and Don't-you-remember
is a game for passing hours.

Somewhere between Truth
Or Consequences, New Mexico,
and the Indian school in Browning,
history slips silently by,
leaving only its poisoned blankets.
The buffalo hunters are all gone
and the log trucks are permanently parked
outside the Cascade Cafe
where philosophy is free
and grim and the paint
is stained from leaks. Bad coffee
comes cheap and there's a simple solution
for everything under the sun.

You stop for gas in Barstow or Nogales,
and the sky turns blazing orange.
You scrape the bugs from your windshield
and slip back onto a road
running straight into the darkness,
an old tune summoning a time
when you still loved—was it—
your second wife,

and kids clung to your knees.
Now they are grown. But all that
falls away behind the glare
of headlights on a hill or a passing cattle-car,
erased by the steady whine of wheels.

You drive through Boise, Butte, or Blaine,
coffee in Nisqually, a truck stop john
in Ellensburg or Drain. By midnight,
they all smell the same:
urine, tar and oil and diesel exhaust, and coffee
that tastes of Styrofoam.

On the loneliest bleak nights
in the heart of the American west,
you can drive all night forever
and no matter how far you get,
you wake up again in the west,
the landscape constantly changing,
but always so vast that everyone is alone
and history is a bad novel you can close
whenever you need a good night's sleep
or the general oblivion of Holiday Inn.

Then the meadowlark signs up first light. Or you hear
the mockingbird or a mourning dove and know
it is a desert at your feet, the road
already dancing in the heat,
distant hills transparent,
shimmering in waves.

Or a tired hawk
scowls from his perch on a split-rail fence,
then rises on effortless wings,
crucified against the sky,
high damp mountain air
carrying the odor of ammonia
up from the pasture below.

Up the last canyons, crossing the Great Divide,
there will be snow.

5.
In the middle of the afternoon, my paramour
pauses with her wheelbarrow load
of freshly dug iris bulbs
destined for the compost heap
and asks, What now?

"Simplify. Simplify."
I repeat it like a mantra.

I do not despise my ex-wife's iris
nor her foxglove nor her plague
of wild violets,
but they must go.

Here, I'll plant a lace-leaf maple;
there, a Japanese iris and a pale lily
in a bed of moss in the shade. The rose
was eaten by passing deer,
but its stubble will remain and maybe grow.

Prune the English ivy, the clematis,
and this thorny stuff that grows along the wall.
Dig out the weeping cherry
and cut a wide path
through the turf leading to the studio we'll build.
We'll buck six cords of wood from the trees we fell.

And as evening comes, we pause again together.
The slash pile crackles and smokes.
Somewhere in the dusk, a few frogs
begin to sing frog-love songs.
Rivulets of sweat run down Gray's face as she grins.

Her shirt, knotted below her breasts,
is plastered to her chest. High overhead,
a nighthawk darts and cries.
I open her shirt and we stretch
our aching bodies in the grass to cool.

Another sun drowns in the west. A wall
of light fog descends through the woods,
pushing inland from the strait.

I roll on my side and inch
slowly down her body, kissing breasts and belly,
and lay my head on her thigh.

A few feet away, at the edge of the grass,
a salamander moves even more slowly
into shadows beneath a rotting cedar stump.
A faint breeze raises goose bumps
on Gray's damp skin

and makes her nipples pucker.
I rise and cover her body
with my body,
hugging her close for warmth.
She tastes of salt and longing.
I kiss her and she shivers.

We lie naked in our garden,
sweaty, chilly, exhausted,
and make lazy love against the night
while the first stars come on
like porch lights
blinking down a highway,
unwinding a timeless river.

6.
As if the water would answer, I go on talking.
I am telling the waves the story of my days,
entering my plea
at the tribunal of the sea, walking alone
along the beach at Kalaloch.

Here I once made love with a woman I adored
while a lonely figure watched
from distant bluffs high above,
and the gray implacable tide drew away
to meet the gray implacable sky.

Our cries, love or death, were drowned
by the cries of wandering gulls.

Now a year has passed. And still, he is there, watching
from the shadows, sighing the sighs of the sea.

Memory, like waves. Stained with the salts of desire,
a shoreline creature talking fear away,
I go on confessing to the water,
understanding only that the final sentence is death,

a mist falling over the moon
that is the signature of all things,
beautiful and empty
as the solitary seed syllable of the loon.

What the Water Knows

What the mouth sings, the soul must learn to forgive.
A rat's as moral as a monk in the eyes of the real world.
Still, the heart is a river
pouring from itself, a river that cannot be crossed.

It opens on a bay
and turns back upon itself as the tide comes in,
it carries the cry of the loon and the salts
of the unutterably human.

A distant eagle enters the mouth of a river
salmon no longer run and his wide wings glide
upstream until he disappears
into the nothing from which he came.

Only the thought remains. Lacking the eagle's cunning
or the wisdom of the sparrow, where shall I turn,
drowning in sorrow? Who will know what the trees know,
the spidery patience of young maple or what the willows confess?

Let me be water. The heart pours out in waves.
Listen to what the water says.
Wind, be a friend.
There's nothing I couldn't forgive.

Three Stitches

I sat and listened
to nothing. And then, somewhere,
an alder leaf fell.

•

Now summer begins,
the woods, the sky, even dreams—
all tinged yellow green

•

In the spider's lair,
the struggling mosquito finds
its own true nature

To Gary Snyder

Nearly forty years
have passed since Kenneth Rexroth
introduced me to
the mountains and rivers of
your poems, the campfire light

flickering softly
across a page of Milton,

animal shadows
and wide, wise innocent eyes
observing from the darkness.

I was just a kid
with a heroin habit
and a talent for
self-destruction. Your poems
returned me to sanity—

as much as could be
at the time. Now poor Kenneth
has been fifteen years
in his grave, whose epitaph
I set and printed in his

The Silver Swan some
twenty years ago, not long
before your *Gaia*.
"Above Pate Valley," yellowed
with age and writ in a hand

imitating yours,
still remains in my office,
along with snapshots
of Kenneth in the Cascades
circa nineteen twenty-eight.

I no longer go
deep into the mountains, but
remember printing
your "Axe Handles" every time
I buck wood. Which is to say

nine bows to a friend
and teacher who encouraged
a lifetime's study.

The mountains are in my heart,
and all the rivers that flow

flow from headwaters
"going back roughly forty
thousand years, dating
from the early cave paintings,"
you remarked in Alaska

twenty years ago;
and, "About five thousand years
is all one human
mind can comfortably hold."
You've managed to redefine

civilization.
You have given us Stone Age
economics and
the idea of *practice*—
Buddhist and/or poetic—

you have given me
a model for my practice,
not something merely
to imitate, but a wise
counsel culled from the ages.

Now I'm no longer
young, though plentifully foolish—
my Japanese friends
have dubbed me *Obaka-san*—
and you're almost old enough

to be the tribal
elder you have always been.
"Mountains and rivers
without end." From an old scroll,
a single kernel of thought

blossoms forty years
from its inception, like that
hundred-and-twenty-
year cycle of some bamboo.
The poem becomes the life

in some respects, it
deepens our engagement with
all that is human,
with all this temporal world,
plagued by all-too-human greed.

Who will join Shiva
and Tara, Kokopelli
and Dōgen Zenji in
"the dance of the intellect
among the ten thousand things?"

What I want to say,
what I have struggled to say
in this poem, is
that you have been a master
and model, a friend and sage

for those who follow.
And if I may paraphrase:
That's what a poet
is—one who recognizes
sacramental relationships.

That is the real work—
reading books or bucking wood
or washing babies—
attentive lives all our days:
the real joy is gratitude.

To Adrienne Rich

How much you have changed
my life! It is breathtaking
to look back again
on the deep sickness of men
of my grim generation.

You scared us witless
often enough with your bold
commitment to truth
and uncommon decency.
I still know the man I was,

one who raised his hand
or voice against the very
thing he loved the most—
the sickness of self gnawing
away inside like a dog.

The answers I found,
I found as often as not
within your poems
and essays, or in Atwood's,
or in Simone de Beauvoir.

Poetry readings
against the Vietnam War
were everywhere, but
I was already a vet
and had become a C.O.

and still that sickness
waged war within me—to be
what, if not a man?

You brought me to see that grief,
like hope, belongs to us all.

What diminishes
a woman makes a man small
in equal degree.
More than thirty years have passed
since I first offered shelter

for battered women.
My wife opened a shelter
twenty years ago.
And yet the murders continue,
day after horrible day.

And despite it all,
we find peace at the center.
You have changed my world
and my perception of it
finally and forever.

Orphaned in this world,
I was born to this struggle:
a lifetime searching
for kinship, for becoming,
for endless transformation.

This revolution
has no beginning, no end.
What I most value
is most easily attained:
sustenance and gratitude.

"Gratitude" is such
a simple word, a verbal bow
I make with palms clasped,

Gasshō! "Yours with the Buddha."
"I dreamed you were a poem,"

you wrote a lover,
and I often think you, too,
are a long poem
whose gift is the gift of change,
of sublime transformation—

"If you're not part of
the solution," we all said,
"you are the problem."
And that's still as true today.
Your poetry *is* a Way.

"The poet today,"
you wrote in 'seventy-four,
"must be twice-born. She
must have begun as a poet,
she must have understood

the suffering of
the world as political, . . .
and on the other
side of politics she must
be reborn again as a

poet." To be born
again and yet again is
the poet's foremost
obligation. Audre Lorde
said it: "Poetry is not

a luxury." It
is lifesaving, sustaining
what can't otherwise
be salvaged from the wreckage
of the American life.

After Coltrane's "I'll Get By"

These autumn nights I think hard and long
on Wang Wei, ancient Chinese poet alone,
resigned behind his brushwood gate,
nothing at his door but the wind,
the same white clouds and mountains.

My old dog groans in his sleep.
The cold October moon fills my room with light.
I light a cigarette and pour a shot of tequila,
promising myself I'll clean up my act
next week.

Neither drunk nor sober,
something of Coltrane lingers
long after the music's over,
something of the loneliness that transcends loneliness,
like the emptiness of Wang Wei.

It tends to get very late.
Opening a book, I read a poem
in a voice that rasps in the night.
"A wretch needs his wretchedness," Roethke cried.
All right, all right. I'll go to bed.

I got to be up
to greet the light.

Seattle Spring

After ninety-four
consecutive days of rain,
even frogs don't sing.

"One Who Studies the Past in Order to
Learn the Present Is Fit to Teach."
For Emily Troutman, archivist
9th day, 11th month, 4698, Year of the Iron Dragon

K'ung-fu Tzu walked by the dynastic temple,
mourning the death of his friend, Yen Hui.
Perhaps he meditated on Lao Tzu's
"Beauty and ugliness have one origin,"

and asked himself whether virtue did not
likewise rise from a root. His old friend
had struggled to be a virtuous man.
There were dark clouds on the horizon.

A disciple, Tzu Kung, wanted to lift
his master's spirit, but K'ung-fu Tzu turned away.
"No one knows me," he said. "They call me,
'that dog from a house in mourning.'"

Tzu Kung asked, "How can you say such a thing?"
I thought of such things this morning,
a little frightened and embarrassed by
one who has looked into my history.

How will time judge me? Damned if I know.
My accomplishment is, I got up today.
I tried to write a poem. K'ung-fu Tzu said,
"The study of the low penetrates the high."

To Hayden Carruth

I.
Pilate asks, "What is
love?" For which I substitute

174

friendship, which is love
unburdened by erotic
passion, but informed by love's

kindliness, if not
by the inevitable
necessities of
dialectic argument.
And so I begin again—

"My dear friend," I say,
meaning I have stood breathless
before the severe
beauty and anguish and love
and delight in your poems,

stood breathlessly still
as I listened to the turn
of a line or phrase
or flinched in recognition
of a painful truth revealed.

I do not know why
we must do it, why the line
begins somewhere in-
side the mind, its insistent
music delivering us

into another
world where the poem unfolds
from within, telling
us what's really on our minds.
I swear it is so. I've sworn

allegiance before—
not to some bloody old flag
snapping in the wind,

and certainly not to that
junkyard dog, the Patriot—

but to what can be
found in poetry: friendship
and small dignities,
evidence of a long life
lived with an ear to the wind

and a heart exposed.
I swear it's always been so.
A heart or poem
cannot be closed completely.
The heart of Herakleitos

or Euripedes,
like the rhythms of Sappho,
resounds in your lines
as surely as the weather
of an age. And so I go

there in search of the
old familiar, the trusted
thing, the poem as
continuing thread binding
friend to friend across centuries.

Friendship is solace,
the root of a good marriage.
I extend my hand,
unwashed, still bloody with all
the excesses of our age.

I stand before your
poems as before a great
hearth in deep winter,

comforted by your labors.
I find sanctuary here.

We have our Pilates'
clean hands in public office.
We have messiahs
aplenty. I'm sick to death
of all those who want glory.

Poetry may change a life
or burn white hot with passion;
it may bring a smile
or be a coat for Jacob
wandering the wilderness,

but you and I know
that lust for fame is folly.
You ought to have a
Nobel Prize, a Pulitzer,
all the honors in the world.

But that is not why
you write. For which act my heart
goes out to you who
helped me learn to open it.
For which act you are my friend

forever, doing
the real work of poetry.
Fuck money. Fuck fame.
There are three worlds. In this one,
gratitude flows like honey.

The suffering world
brings about its own demise.
This world is neither

fair nor wise, but paradise
reveals itself in every line.

What, finally, *is* love?
Willingness to face the end
without blinking? The
gift made—and given freely.
I bow to the poem, my friend.

2.
Wily Su Tung-p'o
observed of Wang Wei's landscapes,
"All of his paintings
contain poems; all of his
poems contain the essence

of paintings." Thus said,
he pointed toward balance
to find harmony.
In one inch of snow, tulip
bulbs at Kage-an frozen,

the woodpile a block
of ice to be chipped with my
splitting maul, little
raccoon tracks around the back
door and down the frozen steps

and off into woods
that creak with the shift of winds,
I attend my chores,
muttering against the cold
furies of northern winter.

You who love the snow
can have it. And you can have
the chainsaw poems

and marvelous descriptions
of Nor'east country townsfolk

in all their glory.
Just send me the warmth of rain.
"Sin is not so much
knowing (if it were, every-
body would be innocent)

as wanting to know."
Thus you quote Camus on sin.
I suppose my sin
has been relentless wanting
to know, whereas what I want

most to know right now
is comfort in married life,
the garden in spring,
the work at hand. This bloody,
bitter weather gets me down.

In my sins are all
my virtues, in my virtues
all my sins, for which
I can make no excuses:
I balance above the abyss.

This landscape is etched
in my blood—wouldn't have it
any other way.
This snow won't last, and neither,
happily, will you or I.

So I turn to your
cold weather poems, your thoughts
on sin and virtue
or on temporality.
Not for comfort exactly,

but because the truth
of the matter is, like that
other Williams—Hank—
I get so doggone lonesome—
and there you are, with woodsmoke,

almost three-quarters
of a century, and yet
the poems go on,
footsteps leading through the snow
until they become the snow.

You, like Su Tung-p'o,
are a master, a wily
old fox in the storm,
footsteps leading through the snow
until they become the snow.

3.
Reading your *Scrambled
Eggs and Whiskey*, I took note:
"The great poems of
our elders in many tongues
we struggled to comprehend

who now are content
with mystery simple and
profound . . ." and isn't
that the greatest mystery
of all? That we can at last

find within ourselves
a mundane ecstasy, or
simple contentments
known only in poverty
and at the price of patience—

which isn't my strong
suit, or so I always thought
until I awoke one day
and—sure enough—white whiskers
on a wizened, tired face.

Only then did I
begin to realize what I'd believed
all along: that joy
is not the orgasmic cry
in the night, nor lovely sighs

following after—
which are a mystery them-
selves, albeit thin
and fragile as a moth's wing
in flickering candlelight—

I wrote of Tu Fu
years ago, "His joys were neither
large nor many, but
they were precise." A moment
of prescience perhaps? Or
just the inevitable

result of struggling
to comprehend the tongue of
such a great master?
Probably both. In such great
and noble struggle I come

face-to-face with my
own small, quiet ecstasies
over a poem
that says for me what I could
not otherwise find true words

to say. Carruth or
Tu Fu, Sappho, Seferis—
it doesn't matter:
the poem somehow reveals
its particularities

and I am brought down
to my knees in gratitude
for the gift received.
If I am content at all,
it is because I struggled

all those many years,
because I was so foolish
then as to believe
that poetry was enough
to teach me to live, to love.

Sisyphus
To Hayden Carruth and Jim Harrison

It's strange, isn't it,
waking up to realize
one day that you've gone
over the hill, as they say,
and are facing the short side

of your string of days—
as Chuang Tzu aptly put it—
and then you begin
to face, not urgency, not
fear of death, but real comfort

in saying, "So this
is what I've become, this is

the man I am and
now I can take it easy,"
except that there ought to come

a time when the last
trace of last night's moon shining
in the water won't
move us to the edge of tears,
free of Sisyphean tasks,

when a beautiful
woman is not enough to
bring us dutifully
to our knees, or when the need
to undulate with warblers

floating on a breeze
is enough to make you scream.
Sisyphus was young.
He pushed the huge stone of self
until he became undone.

Even the stories
are sweeter for the young—who
drink too deeply
often enough and wander
in a semi-drunken state

of equal parts bliss
and all seven deadly sins.
In a warm spring rain,
the first cherry blossoms fall,
covering the path like snow.

Issa would be pleased.
I wouldn't be young again
for any damned thing.

Here's Mathios Paskalis
still among those Greek roses,

and, Seferis says,
his nose has grown wrinkled while
his pipe keeps smoking
as he descends the stone steps
that never come to an end.

I am beginning
at last to understand what
Seferis really
meant when he said, "I want
no more than to speak simply,

to be granted that
grace." Simplicity's the end,
just a period
at the end of a compound
complex sentence, the great stone

of Sisyphus seen
from the hill's other side.
Let old men converse
across the abyss of time. We'll
watch salamanders couple

in a green pool's shade
and remember the passions
we indulged when we
were forty-five. Old age comes
more quickly than Yangtze floods.

And it's not all bad.
We can set a sturdy pace.
When there's nothing left

to prove, simplicity is
the very nature of things.

Chuang Tzu's fisherman
brought Confucius to his knees.
To follow the way,
he says with his sly grin, is
to finally reach completion.

Which is not an end,
but a means. Sisyphean
tasks, like lost causes,
are the only ones worthwhile.
And then the robin sings.

To Hayden Carruth on His Eightieth Birthday

Jesus, Hayden, it's hard to believe you're
eighty. When I began reading your work
forty years ago, how could I have known
that you were forty and forty is so young?
And how could I have ever guessed that I,
a young marine in Japan, might become
your student, your editor, your friend?

The way of poetry is mysterious,
indeed, as we discover each time we rise
into its occasion. And in the end,
it doesn't matter that we suffered or
did not suffer for our art, but that we
found in verse the courage to stand against
the state, political and religious.

How often you've said you don't know a thing
about Zen or the Tao, but you're a sage

all the same, and in the tradition of
Chuang Tzu and Confucius, a questioner,
a loner who has struggled to reach out.
And now to your Whitmanic beard, our bard
of existential grit, I raise my cup:

I wouldn't wish another eighty years
on anyone, but may you live a thousand,
and a thousand generations more. You
have shown me my way, and others their own.
You have praised what others scorned
and embraced essential *mu,* the emptiness of Zen.
Ten years ago, you wrote, "All old men are fools,"

and I thought, "Ryōkan might have said that,
or maybe Yeats, or Ez in his old age,"
and laughed because it's true and getting truer
with the accumulation of my days.
You have no pride, and oh, how I admire that.
What does not change is change. Your way's my way.
In poetry, even the fool grows wise. Nine bows.

To Bill and Kris

I never wanted
a cell phone or electric
mail, a Cadillac
or a limousine to cruise
the Information Highway.

A dusty back road
through obdurate relics of
civilization

is where I've built my retreat.
Give me a California

Job Drawer, a press
I can ink by hand, cotton
fiber paper made
by hand in France, Italy
or Japan, and let me be.

I like the feel of
the poem as it takes shape
in my hands, the smell
of damp paper, oil, type wash,
the hum and clunk of the press.

Technology is,
of itself, neither good nor
evil, but bequeaths
and reveals what's in the heart
already: whether pine breeze

or voracious
appetite. It's not that I
reject the comforts
of modern technology—
I want my running water,

electricity,
a warm house in deep winter.
More is not better—
not always. The marketplace
attracts a gaggle of thieves.

Rats seek the rice bowl.
I've spent a lifetime getting
a little out of

line, content with solitude,
half a recluse, a throwback,

building with my hands
this little Buddhist retreat
we named Kage-an,
Shadow Hermitage, under
the dark cedars of the North-

west coast. This is not
"a retreat from the world's ways,"
as some Buddhists think,
but an entryway, a door
opening on the real world.

I keep things simple
in my hands and heart. I was,
from the start, a fool—
stubborn, happy in my work,
making a gift no one wants

and giving it all
away. I still remember
the first time I heard
a single alder leaf fall
through autumn trees, a "click, click"

as it tumbled down.
You can't give away that sound.
You can hold the moon
between your hands, but you can't
hold it long. The simple fact

of poetry is
astonishment enough. That
and life's ironies
duly noted as I write
this epistle on my Mac.

Song and Dance
For William O'Daly on his fiftieth birthday

1. *Salutation*

Our way was, from the start,
altogether clear. And no apology.

No praise. No blame.
No shame. No glory.

In love with learning,
we yearned to burn brightly.

In those lines we memorized—
Levertov, Creeley, Carruth, Kinnell—

lay a kind of redemption, modest
salvation from the savagery of war.

Milton by firelight while a war raged on,
Jeffers, Pound and peyote.

How could I have guessed that you'd become
Neruda's second skin, a Chinese novelist?

I didn't know my name.
Thirty years have quickly passed,

little wisdom earned at the expense
of our mutual blissful ignorance

and indolence—we still believe in poesy.
I roar with laughter when I think of you

and me, and of all our wonderfully
embarrassing stupidities.

2. *Jig Tune*

"Lend me a hand," I said to my friend
in nineteen seventy-one.

I said it again in 'seventy-two,
"What you could help me do . . ."

and all these years rushed past—
"only the affection lasts"—

and then another echo,
"Bro, can you spare me a minute,

a glass of wine and a little time
to salve a gaping wound?"

Memory revises the tunes.
Half my life, more than half

of yours, and what's in store
but a little bit more—

"Bro, can you hear my blues?"
"Hey! What club do I use?"

So many songs, so many voices—
the bardic, the tragic, the harpie—

each making choices,
each with its own bad timing.

All the same, right or wrong,
the rope is made strong

by the character of its twining.

Weasel, Crow, and Coyote on the Dharma Trail

A weasel went out
one day and saw a large crow
dancing in the dust.
"Ha-ha," the crow cried, "Ha-ha."
Poor Weasel, not speaking Crow,

thought the old crow
was humiliating him.
"I'll get you for that!"
he barked, "I'll gnaw on your bones!"
Weasel crouched low in the grass

and slowly crept close.
But when he made his great leap,
he came up with dust.
"I'll get you for that!" he barked,
retreating into shadows.

Crow bobbed on his bough.
"Ha-ha, ha-ha," he bellowed.
Weasel leaped again,
snapping the air with his jaws,
"You arrogant prick!" he screamed,

"I'll get you for that!"
Far off, another crow called,
"What's all the ruckus?"
Crow chuckled and replied, "Just
stupid Weasel eating dust.

I tried to warn him
about Coyote," Crow called,
"but all he wanted
was to eat me, then got mad
when I escaped. What a fool!"

Weasel slunk away
with his tail between his legs.
Crow called Coyote,
"Hey, old friend, here comes Weasel,
all tired out from meanness.

I tried to warn him,
but he's too mean to listen."
Coyote grinned. He
licked his chops and sniffed the air.
"The angry ones are easiest."

Why Crows are Noisy
After the Sanskrit

Darkness swallows even the sun.
Afraid they too will vanish,
darkness into darkness,

crows at daybreak
shout, "Crow! Crow!"

Rising
December 24, 1998

"No romance here, but a willingness to age and die at the speed of sound."

       —Jim Harrison

It's time again not to push a metaphor too far,
but when solstice falls on frozen ground
and snow falls steadily on the water, islands
dissolving in the chalky distance,
and only a single crow in the sky,

I think of Yesenin at the doctor's,
finding the old woman whose legs were blue,
Akhmatova so solemn at the gates,
Tu Fu huddled over his charcoal stove,
trying to thaw his fingers enough
to hold his writing brush. Bashō listened
in the silence to ice crack his rice jar.
The sky is slate white—a chalkboard
erased ten thousand times.

Winter solstice. Nothing inherently holy
in that, except the days grow longer now,
the cold a little less cold because it comes
on the wings of spring. It's Ramadan, Chanukah,
Kwanzaa and Christmas, and for a moment,
the missiles have been silenced. The world
is strangely still, trees black against the sky.
Hayden's alone in his little house in the eastern cold
as I am alone in mine, a continent away.
He writes of dialing 911:
"A helicopter ride would be fun."

Li Po looked up at a pale, thin moon
and raised his sake cup. Not much has changed.
Those who claim to know murder those
they call false prophets while science
improves their tools. There is death
in Jerusalem, frozen death among the homeless
all across the heartland. A president
is impeached, and the stock market rises.
Tibet is Chinese and the Makah want whales.

I got up from my *zafu* in the first gray light
and blew out the candle and went into the kitchen
and turned on the lights; I made a latte
and went outside and stood
shivering on the deck in the last of the dark,

remembering ten thousand dawns I watched
emerge from trees and mountains.

I remembered my wife rushing in from the garden,
"Let's go make love—the dragonflies are fucking!"
What man was I when I cleared this land
and built my hermitage? What man today?
I remembered the dogs I buried.
Slowly, a few snowy trees turned from dark to white.
This world is frost on an old man's breath,
memory rushing into memory.

Twenty years ago, on a warm midsummer night,
Gary Snyder got up on stage at the Town Tavern,
beer mug in hand, and recited "Ode to the West Wind"
in his indelibly lovely voice
to a boisterous, cheering crowd. It made me
feel alive at the speed of sound. Outside,
the same moon rose above the water
that Wang Wei watched rise over the river
a thousand years before. It was the same night.
It was the same poem.

Lost in Translation

Olav Hauge wrote, "Read Lu Chi
and make a poem." Robert Hedin
sits alone in the dark, translating
Hauge's poem. At my desk, alone
in the hours before dawn, I read
Hedin reading Hauge reading Lu Chi,
whom I translated twenty years ago,
learning to make a poem.

Hauge, knowing no Chinese,
brings another, unnamed, guest

to our little conflagration.
Whom was Hauge reading?
Who knows, who knows?
First gray light and August rain
fall gently through the trees.
I'll tell my poem to the crows.

To W. S. Merwin

And then there are my
Followers, mad for a bit of color,
Damn them . . .

I have followed you, William,
through decades of transformation—
yours, mine, your poems'—
until I have entered this
colorful autumn of life,

and you have grown old
with tenderness and wisdom.
I remember stars
high over California
beaches where I read *The Lice*.

I loved to recite
"The Drunk in the Furnace" to
students drunk on words
and dreams of being poets.
There was a war raging on,

and I believed we
could have a hand in stopping
such stupid bloodshed.
Poetry would be my way,
and you were more my teacher

than the little men
who called themselves professors.
You were in my ears
and heart and eyes all those days,
like California weather,

sky so blue, so bright
I'd hardly believe my eyes.
I believed the words
that opened a door on a world.
I would be alone, then,

in my long struggle
against the utter darkness,
alone with myself
in constant transformation.
You were my own magician.

You showed me a way.
You gave me to poetry.
There'd be no Copper
Canyon Press today, except
you showed me my way.

What can a poet,
any poet, be true to,
but one's own vision?
Devotion and commitment,
not to the literary,

but to the calling,
the avocation that makes
transformation so
very necessary. And
I mean that literally.

You have changed my life
by being true to your words.

Old friend, old master,
I too love our conversations.
They, like poems, are too rare.

And yet I am here,
your words in my heart and ears
as you go under
the knife. I've given my life
to what I have learned from you

and just a few others.
If I were religious,
I would pray for you.
But I am not. I offer
the testament of a fool,

a poem of love
to a great elder brother
I barely know, but
have known almost forever.
Get well. You are a treasure.

In Memoriam, Morris Graves

Rising from my *zafu* just as dawn breaks
over the trees, below a few thin clouds
that will burn off in an hour, I'm pleased
cherry and plum trees bloom, daffodil flowers
falling or fallen, and the garden glows
in various shades of yellow and green.
This house I built so long ago grows old.
The garden and the life are a poem
evolving from traditions old as time.
I came here green, unwise. I'm still unwise.
Like the old Buddhist poets who taught me
how to live, I believe the poem is

a sacramental act, pure devotion
to whatever may be revealed only
through the music of intuition. The
dance of the intellect, the dance of wild
imagination, illuminates what
cannot otherwise be known—a koan,
one's rational and irrational mind
at one. It is so because leaves are green,
and death is born in greenness; and it's true
as blue and right as rain, and sustains me
in my practice. As Carolyn Kizer
remarked on Chinese poetry, wisely,
"It teaches us the value of friendship.
And you may not believe it, but that's far
more important than husbands, wives, even
children. Because what are you if you are
not first of all a friend?"
                                        So now I turn
in my fifty-eighth year to face Tu Fu,
who died, in exile, at my age. And, "I
have beaten out my exile," Ezra wrote
in a hard time years before Rapallo.
My exile is not alienation,
but rootedness, poetry's sustenance.
My daily friends are robins listening
for worms, busy finches, jays, noisy crows,
a woodpecker now and then. And Morris,
who painted the wind. "The painting has no
narrative. It is exactly what it is,
flowers and light." And the poem has no
paraphrase, but embodies what it is—
found only in its singing. The *cante
jondo*, "to keep bitterness from sorrow."
I will not mourn the death of one so true.
I raise my cup and bow and make this song
because a few friends have sustained me,
and embody what poetry has taught me.

For Kyra Gray O'Daly
Born October 10, 1997

Yellow maple leaves
are already falling through
baby Kyra's tears

All Here
For Ella Addison Wiegers, b. xi:99

Body of dew, mind
of empty sky—the prelude
and the afterword

•

Under bare willows,
pond frogs sing about old age
while girls dream of princes

Midsummer

Two yearling deer
stood in heavy falling mist
in the middle of

the road leading in-
to town, brown coats glistening,
huge eyes open wide,

caught in the headlights
in the first yellowish smear
of coming daybreak.

Twenty feet away,
I finally stopped the car
and sat still inside,

eyes locked together
in a curious searching
with those of the doe.

Minute by minute,
we were transfixed, motionless,
each imagining

the other. And then
the sun peeled back the dark clouds
like a second skin,

and, in unison,
the deer stepped slowly forward,
gently, cautiously,

off the road, into
underbrush that flourishes
along the woods' edge

and vanished in mist.
Dazed, I returned to my day,
to the work at hand.

And now, the hour late
in the morning, mist falling
again, I can still

feel my skin prickle
under those beautiful brown
doe-eyes searching me

like a lover's hand,
cautious, slowly exploring
something deep in me

I cannot touch or name.

Seducing the Sparrow

Birds live in a world without karma.
—Morris Graves

Why must the noble rose
bristle before it blooms, and why
must the frost declare
allegiance to the dew?

Don't tell me the robin's
forlorn invitation
could not be denied.
I've heard the magpie's lies.

Outside my window,
twenty-seven juncos
consort in a cedar tree,
fat and happy to be free

of all desire—ah, but
that's not true! See
how they dance and turn
when I throw out the seed.

New Math
Epithalamion for Nina and John

When two become one,
that one is greater than two—
how could anyone
otherwise surrender such
indecorous quantities

of greed as are in-
vested in the pronoun *I*,
subordinating
self for that which is plural?
Ryōkan points at this bright moon

and knows his finger
and the moon and this long night
make one. The marriage
is born of nuptials, plural,
the exchange of mutual vows

born in the Latin
nuptiae—also plural—
many vows making
one ceremony—wedding—
making the one of many.

This from *nubere*,
the taking of a husband.
And *husband*? —from the
old Norse *husbondi*, the house-
dweller, the conservator.

And wife is a *wyf*,
a "veiled one," embodiment
of the mystery

that makes of the plural one,
her secrets revealed only

to the husbandman
with whom she builds the temple
that is a garden
witnessed in the *Song of Songs*
through centuries of devotion.

We become the sum
of all we can give away.
The garden and the
gardeners, the soil and sun,
love and labor: all make one.

The Orchid Flower

Just as I wonder
whether it's going to die,
the orchid blossoms

and I can't explain why it
moves my heart, why such pleasure
comes from one small bud
on a long spindly stem, one
blood red gold flower

opening at mid-summer,
tiny, perfect in its hour.

Even to a white-
haired craggy poet, it's
purely erotic,

pistil and stamen, pollen,
dew of the world, a spoonful

of earth, and water.
Erotic because there's death
at the heart of birth,

drama in those old sunrise
prisms in wet cedar boughs,

deepest mystery
in washing evening dishes
or teasing my wife,

who grows, yes, more beautiful
because one of us will die.

Organic Form

A year on one line,
searching for the poetry:
outside, breezes rise—
spring to summer to autumn—
leaves fall, rot, and feed the tree.

Little Epic Elegy
Denise Levertov (1923–1997)

She is gone who brought
us closer to what we are,
who brought us a world—
a passion for the garden,
a heaven of moons and stars.

And now she attends
our days with the salts of truth
and all the honeys
of conviction. Her vision
returns us into a world

of mystery, awe,
all compassion and delight,
to joy in the work
of being fully human,
always picking up the torch,

passing on the light.

Not Meaning, but Being
For Jim Farmer

In the darkening last days of October,
I stand in fog and drizzle, under the great trees,
splitting maul in hands that a week ago
held golf clubs on a warm bright autumn afternoon.

Splitting the wood, building the fire,
I think of the fire in my belly over a round of golf,
which, like Zen, is about character and nothingness.
I enjoy the company of few men. Solitude

has always been my way. But now, as the year
begins to close, I think of the comfort
I have known along the fairways with a man
who shares my passion for the game.

My wife would ask, "How's Jim?"
"Fine," I'd say, and she'd ask, "What did you talk about?"
And I'd say truthfully, "Nothing. Nothin' much.
We just played golf." But of course there were things said,

mostly unimportant because the matter at hand
was a five iron or a putter, deep rough or
that one clean perfect swing that always
brings us back again. Golf is about nothing,

I suppose. Like a life reflected on, it's nothing
but what we bring to it. "Meaning" has
little meaning in the end. And yet we love
and live and work and play and die

within the borders of that grand nothing
that lies at the heart of things. What
did we talk about? Nothing. Nothing
at all. Because he is my friend.

A Woodsplitter's Meditation

1.

Early October mist pours through the trees
surrounding Kage-an, bringing autumn
chills that send me out to the woodpile with
my new splitting maul. I test it simply,
popping dry alder I cut two years ago.

Two stellar jays come to see, yammering
loudly from the low boughs of a cedar tree
grown tall from a nurse log. I split hemlock,
spruce and fir I bucked last winter. Each pops
open like a book, pages glued with sap.

I have read this book, and so have the jays.
It is written in ordinary days
and deeds addressing all temporal desire.
I laugh too, then go in and light the fire.

2.

I began this poem a month ago,
then put it in a drawer. Since then I've been
to California and seen Hood Canal
canopied with orange and yellow maple.
Autumn chill turned to early winter cold.

My bones grow stiffer as I grow older,
but I do as well as I am able.
I heard my friend's husband died suddenly,
leaving me, bad habits and all, mourning,
and, being his elder, feeling guilty.

Time is beauty, I think sometimes. I love
these last brown leaves as I love growing old,
sowing last month's plantings, tending this day's
business at the woodpile, facing the snow.

3.

I have no wisdom to ease her mourning.
I have no wisdom at all. I carry
the wood I split and build fires in the night,
and huddle in my skin. What do I know?
Leaves fall, trees grow. The snow is magical.

Time is beauty. Time together, time apart.
The woodsplitter's meditation contains
no answers, only questions, and seeks the heart
of what time makes us: rings and scars, bruisings
and vows and destinies never imagined.

What can I know of anyone's loss? I
invest in the certainty of my death,
no time to squander and no need to rush,
but when she asks, "Where shall I turn?" I'm hushed.

4.

Shall I say Li Ch'ing-chao mourned beautifully?
That Yuan Chen's great elegies are great
because he speaks so simply? I'm silent
because my ignorance overwhelms me—
I bow to what I cannot understand.

The *Upāya* teaches "skillful means," the
Kannon long life sutra means compassion,
the loud cracks of my splitting maul recite
a hundred temple bells, a hundred sutras.
For whom? For what, without a little heat?

I will tell her I have not learned to grieve
as a widow grieves, and what will it mean?
The wood crib full, the fire lit, I sit
alone in dying light and slowly breathe.

To Amy, before Her Wedding

Thirty years ago,
on a sunny August day,
I married my muse.

I did. And the vow I made
then rings as true today as

ever. I waited
fifty years for marital
bliss. I sat in the

utter emptiness alone,
alone as we each must be

before we can give
ourselves away. Then I gave
it all away and

found myself a wife to love
who understands my practice.

"Practice makes perfect,"
my piano teacher said
when I was a boy.

Practice is everything
according to Hui Neng-tzu.

That is why I try
today not to try to write

the poem I'd like
to write for you—because I
must empty myself of self

before I can see
even the simplest of truths.
Hayden's right. Poems

are an act of love writ large,
made permanent by writing.

Here at Kage-an
the shadows quickly grow. What
endures, what flowers,

is only the love we've placed—
tough-minded, big-hearted—within
each and every poem.

Reply to T'ao Ch'ien

June rain drizzles through the heavy boughs
of cedar and spruce and knocks
the blossoms from the cherry trees.
Rhododendron blossoms also fall
as blue irises begin to open.

The bamboo shoots shoot up so quick
I can almost watch them grow.
In the first light of day I sit
in silence, watching one old crow
stalk the borders of the garden.

Whatever truth you told me
in your garden long ago,
it returns, here, now,
in the poem that begins
just beyond its words.

The Goldfinch

The little goldfinch
whammed into the glass door
at full speed:
Thonk! He fluttered,

staggering around the deck
until I opened the door.
Then he flopped into the garden
and scrambled under the house.

When I got down
and peered in at him,
he ruffled his feathers, shook
his head and stepped back.

When I drew back,
he poked his head out,
looked at me wide-eyed,
shuddered, and flew off.

It's wonderful how what we love
can suddenly fly away. I found
on the door when I went back in
a tiny feather in a spot of blood.

Strawberry Picking

Mr. Mitsunaga's strawberry fields
were blistering in August. I worked them
for two years. At two bits an hour, I was
in the money. For a nickel more than my
father paid, I could withstand his fury.
My old man called him, "Mit the Jap," and spat
whenever he said his name. He'd lost friends
in The War, of course, and more in Korea.
McCarthy was in the senate, and I
learned to crawl under my desk in case of bombing.

Mr. Mitsunaga spoke very softly
in his impeccable English. He'd been
to UCLA before Tule Lake.
"Don't hurry," he'd say. "Take time to get it right."

To Yoshinaga Sayuri

What's an old man say
to beautiful roses from
such a great lady?

I was astonished, struck dumb,
my poet's tongue tied numbly.

But it's not roses,
the greatest gift you gave me.
No. It's Sadako.
Folding all her paper cranes.
You gave me a thousand cranes.

You gave me the work
of finding joy making peace.
Sadako, dying,
folding cranes, radiation
consuming her small body—

such joy in sadness,
such sadness in seeking joy.
What our ancestors
have done to one another
cannot ever be excused.

And yet we are here.
Me grateful for your kindness,
silent, embarrassed.
You are a great actress and
a noble human being.

I'm a fool poet
grown white-haired in the shadows
of Hiroshima.
In Chris's shakuhachi,
I felt, I believed, your hand,

but I could not write
the poem for Sadako
afterward. Oh, I
wanted to, I struggled to,
but could not write the poem.

What I cannot write . . .
to . . . for . . . about . . . the victims
of Hiroshima,
I found in Yusuke's father's
carving ten thousand Buddhas.

I found it in you.
Kawabata would be moved
by your elegant
control of consummate grief.
How classically Japanese!

I write this for you
in a Japanese measure,
with just a little
American jazz or blues
contained in every line.

Your roses will bloom
somewhere in my heart and mind
when I fail again.
I too have a crush on you,
one among millions of fans.

Your gift was rarer,
a Buddha smile for the ghost
of a holocaust.
Nine bows, my sensei. Gasshō.
That lesson will not be lost.

The New York Poem

I sit in the dark, not brooding
exactly, not waiting for the dawn
that is just beginning, at six twenty-one,

in gray October light behind the trees.
I sit, breathing, mind turning on its wheel.

Hayden writes, "What use is poetry
in times like these?" And I suppose
I understand when he says, "A poet
simply cannot comprehend
any meaning in such slaughter."

Nevertheless, in the grip of horror,
I turn to poetry, not prose,
to help me come to terms—
such as can be—with the lies, murders
and breathtaking hypocrisies

of those who would lead a nation
or a church. "What use is poetry?"
I sat down September twelfth,
two thousand one in the Common Era,
and read Rumi and kissed the ground.

And now that millions starve
in the name of holy war? Every war
is holy. It is the same pathetic story
from which we derive
"biblical proportion."

I hear Pilate's footsteps ring
on cobblestone, the voice of Joe McCarthy
cursing in the senate, Fat Boy exploding
as the whole sky shudders.
In New York City, the crashes

and subsequent collapses
created seismic waves. To begin to speak
of the dead, of the dying . . . how
can a poet speak of proportion any more
at all? Yet as the old Greek said,

"We walk on the faces of the dead."
The dark fall sky grows blue.
Alone among ash and bones and ruins,
Tu Fu and Bashō write the poem.
The last trace of blind rage fades

and a mute sadness settles in,
like dust, for the long, long haul. But if
I do not get up and sing,
if I do not get up and dance again,
the savages will win.

I'll kiss the sword that kills me if I must.

State of the Union, 2003

I have not been to Jerusalem,
but Shirley talks about the bombs.
I have no god, but have seen the children praying
for it to stop. They pray to different gods.
The news is all old news again, repeated
like a bad habit, cheap tobacco, the social lie.

The children have seen so much death
that death means nothing to them now.
They wait in line for bread.
They wait in line for water.
Their eyes are black moons reflecting emptiness.
We've seen them a thousand times.

Soon the President will speak.
He will have something to say about bombs
and freedom and our way of life.
I will turn the TV off. I always do.
Because I can't bear to look
at the monuments in his eyes.

Poem in the Margins of the *Shōyō Roku*

Yun-yan asked Tao-wu,
"What does the Bodhisattva
of Compassion do
with a thousand hands and eyes?"
"She reaches for the pillow."

"Now I understand:
all over our bodies, then,
there are hands and eyes."
"You got eighty percent." "Oh?"
"Throughout the body—eyes, hands."

The awakened mind
reviles the deluded mind
of moments before.
The emperor's clothes reveal
all that a thief has stolen.

Elegy

From horsetail and catgut,
the high droning wail of the Indian double violin,
part raga, part jazz-blues, a counter-
rhythm rolling through the fingers
on the skin and clay of the tabla . . .

On the dusty banks of the Ganges,
where I have never been but have longed to see,
they are burning the bodies of the dead,
ashes to be carried by the broad brown river
all the way out into the sea.

What's the proper way to mourn
for one who chose to leave this world
against the will of her own monolithic god?
Should Rama Krishna dance?
Should Nikos talk about the songs of Sappho
or Medea and the antiphonies of ancient Greece?

Sometimes whole worlds collide.
The incomprehensibility of infanticide.
I let the wordlessness of these blues
bleed me dry. Blue water, blue sky.
I cannot cry. It is a tragedy old as time,
a sickness deep within the soul.

Black hair, dark eyes, all questioning,
and sorrow still as a crane, figure of long life.
The world's a little smaller when a child dies.
But it will expand again. Already
there are white sails among the islands,
a ferry horn in a wall of fog.

The raga rolls on, summer opening like a door
into a garden on a riverbank whose waters
bear the ashes of the dead downstream,
feeding the garden, feeding us,
while we who love the dead must learn
to live with them in this world of ash and dust.

Nothing Quite So Cold

as a winter night alone,
talking with the dead

Sheepherder Coffee

I used to like sheepherder coffee,
a cup of grounds in my old enameled pot,
then three cups of water and a fire,

and when it's hot, boiling into froth,
a half cup of cold water
to bring the grounds to the bottom.

It was strong and bitter and good
as I squatted on the riverbank,
under the great redwoods, all those years ago.

Some days, it was nearly all I got.
I was happy with my dog,
and cases of books in my funky truck.

But when I think of that posture now,
I can't help but think
of Palestinians huddled in their ruins,

the Afghan shepherd with his bleating goats,
the widow weeping, sending off her sons,
the Tibetan monk who can't go home.

There are fewer names for coffee
than for love. Squatting, they drink,
thinking, waiting for whatever comes.

Summer Rain

I woke past midnight
to the slightly burnt orange odor
of soft summer rain.

My wife slept beside me,
her breath punctuated with
the little sighs of a dreamer.

Outside, pale moonlight
shone through the clouds, the great
evergreens dripping,

the katsura at the far end
of the garden turning
bright yellow already, although

it was early August.
I made a cup of tea and went
out to stand on the deck.

I've clung to this place
like Han Shan-tzu
clung to his cave near the temple

on his beloved mountain.
I've watched these trees reclaim
a chunk of forest—slash,

waste and underbrush
when I came here
thirty years ago.

No place is special
except we make it so
through myth or habitude.

The forest reclaims itself
as best it can. Can I
do less? "No road leads the way,"

Kotarō duly noted, his echo
of Han Shan's echo of Lao Tzu,
and hundreds of years between.

I love beyond words this quiet rain
in these trees, the rose
whose stark white blossom

lasts only a day, this garden
in moonlight, and the woman
who sighs, worried in her dreams

about her sleepless paramour
who rises in the night
to smell the rain.

On Being Asked about Retirement

For most white male Americans my age,
it would be nothing special, I suppose,
to drive an hour to a shopping mall
to buy a summer's clothes.

Year after year I bought a pair of jeans
and a couple of shirts from the discount rack
to mark the beginning of summer.
But suddenly I find myself being paid

for doing just what I've always done—
giving poetry away. Entering
the middle class at my age makes me,
I admit it, nervous. Nevertheless,

I like this Van Heusen, and that Arrow
is awfully nice. I've never owned

a necktie or a suit, and I don't suppose
I'm the least inclined to now.

Put me in a suit and I'd be fake
as a presidential smile. Same old jeans
to greet my day. For an editor,
the crap factor's deep some days.

I'll buy myself some teeth
and a sexy dress for my beautiful wife
and celebrate with *sake* and *unagi,*
and that's a change of life.

It sounds a little odd
to say it this way, but I'm employed
in the service of poetry. I got a job.
And job security.

"Praise a Fool and Make Him Useful"

Now that I've squandered
almost a lifetime going
to school on those old
dead poets who rabble-roused
or retreated into a

kind of solitude
few can understand—now that
I have invested
forty years in the struggle
not to struggle, following

the ancient teachings,
how astonishing it is,
how embarrassing,

to wake up some days and feel—
well—almost respectable.

A Pisan Canto
To Gray Foster

Io fei gibetto a me de le mie case.
                    —*Dante,* Inferno XIII

(PART 1)
You can fly all night above the Atlantic
         in time to see the bluest, brightest dawn emerge as you cross
                  the Alps, wingtips
glinting,
         horizon a blue-yellow haze—
and glide down over green and brown farmlands,
         olive trees in the breeze,
pine trees and olive trees, down
         as the sky grows brighter,
into Milano—

and I, emerging from the bowels of Hades,
         having tasted the Lethe,
emerge from the dark night of my nation,
         from my own darkest night,
bruised by a diffidence that faltered.

But to depart is not
         to depart from the way.
"*Caritas! Caritas!*" my Olga sings,
         bringing the heart of the Greek,
ancient and modern, into her adopted tongue.
         Caritas, Kannon—
a temple is not a business . . .
         Who would betray
a monk's vow of service?

Sail not into an artificial Paradise
        built of fashion and money—
place they crucified Il Duce the second time,
        and who can blame them?
And now another Boss in the White House,
        exporting a fascist state,
man of some fortune
        whose true name will come—
but enter the new old world, old errors repeated,
        Pavese's workers and hookers
rubbing shoulders on a train with lawyers
        in suits that cost more
than my hermitage in the woods.

I am not Odysseus, but a monk in a poet's order,
        a traveler in Toscana, a tourist in Venice.
"Travel not merely to see famous places,
        not merely to appreciate the past,"
the haiku master instructed, "but to learn
        to accept the kindness of strangers."
Such kindness I have known, almost more
        than one can bear,
and suffering also, and
        not a little anger on my journey.

The journey itself is home.

I'll take my coffee in the Piazza
        and learn to say Please and Thank you.
I am not an Ezra, calling upon his gods
        in his hour of desolation,
'though I've desolation in my hour,
        not the panther in the cage,
studying Confucius.

I know Chung Ni, poet that I am,
        I know the master; call me

son of Lu Chi who barred the door—
        two decades on the classics.
Great tragedy of my generation, KR said,
        is that it's no longer possible
to know the poetry of the world.

"To extend one's knowledge to the utmost,"
        Ez sez as K'ung-fu Tzu.
Peace begins only in the heart:
        the poem as koan or case:
the model given is not the answer,
        but provides
a direction: "I will GO to the door/
        I will BE a romantic . . . "
fer instance, Creeley's idiomatic measure
        I put on a blackboard years ago
and challenged the MFAs of a fine institution,
        "Go ahead and scan it."
The great heave to free the American line
        from the dictates of the iamb.
Composition by line because it's more honest
        than the beat of the metronome.
Charlie Olson saw th'advantage
        of the typewriter, first time,
in Saint Liz, visiting Ez, reading a script
        of the Pisan Cantos.

All Romance, from them A-a-a-arabs.
        Bombing the cradle
of civilization, this President smirks,
        translating the Spanish for "shrub"
into "bush," which passes for humor,
        I suppose, in some parts of Texas.
Oil and blood also from the cradle,
        savagely rocking,
man of what god, what destroyer?
        I will *not* surrender my Constitution:

Madison stood for something:
    a little dignity, a little justice
the right to read and speak in peace,
    to follow the romance them A-a-arabs gave us.

And rhyme, too, from the Arabic,
    and the holy calligraphy of the Aleph:
mixed in Provence with French and Italian,
    Langue d'Oc changed western poetry forever.
All born between the Tigris and Euphrates,
    the cradle the Shrub has rocketed.
Drop no bombs on a people
    whose poetry you have not read!
And if your song is not at least
    as beautiful as silence,
keep your mouth shut,
    the Arab proverb says—
traditions brought into English, perfected
    by "our brother Percy"
as he strolled the Arno in Pisa.

And not far from Pisa, nearby in Coltano,
    the home of the DTC,
built by the Fascists to house a fair city
    of Commies and Catholics
who opposed'em, then by the Allies,
    where the panther was caged
and the Pisan Cantos begun.
    Fifteen minutes by car these days
from the noble old Royal Victoria Hotel,
    haunt of Dickens and D'Annunzio
(I read their guest book)
    where Lady Churchill observed,
"The hotel
    is quite adequate."

Fifteen minutes by car,
    across the Arno to narrow roads

canopied by red-barked pine,
    through farmlands with soil
the very color of oil, Piero behind the wheel
    and Alessandro in the back,
offering directions—to Coltano,
    village the size of a thumbnail,
ragged old schoolhouse with rusty gate,
    a mill, the well kept manor
beside the impoverished,
    the smell of last's night rain,
and a tiny store like those in mountain villages
    in Japan, smelt-like fish
soaking in olive oil,
    blocks of cheese, olives,
a pork round, all under glass,
    where we went in for directions.

Immense tragedy
    in the old partisan's stooped shoulders,
but grit in his eye, gravel in his tongue
    when we asked the whereabouts
of the DTC:
    "Are you *fascists*?"
Then, reassured, pointed the way . . .

We walked east and then back, north and then back,
    rich black earth of the fields,
tethered dogs barking, tails wagging,
    long-tailed doves
along the power line—mud everywhere—
    "Fifth element,
MUD, 'sd Napoleon"—
    and you can still smell sweet mint
Ez smelled under his tent flap,
    in his cage, old lion
calling up his gods
    in his hour of desolation,

the poet not yet broken
over "stupid suburban prejudice,"

and here a white horse at roadside
munching lion's tooth, a favorite in salads,
slightly sweet, about the size and shape
of dandelion leaves,
and beyond the fields,
gray marbled clouds over Taishan,
hardly a mountain at all
by Chinese standards—

Chinese standards by which he measured the man,
Legge's *Four Books*, the *Ta Hsueh*,
foremost among them,
great learning
demanding exactitude—
to know the root
and have an orderly mode of procedure—
an orderly mode of procedure
born of respect for one's elders . . .
of finding a noble tradition . . .

Mes frères may speak of justice, *libertá*,
but all dignity is in the deed,
in the friendship or allegiance sustained,
nor is Paradise artificial,
but is one's own good nature.

Odi et amo. Catullo on the banks of the Po
felt the shiv in his back
and lived to tell . . . and lived to sing
his glorious invective.
And another:
Et tu, Brute?
Who would unmake the word's temple?

A grinning daemon
with poisonous charm,
            wearing a mask of Janus.
I woke in a sweat. Who would unmake
            the house of poetry,
who ignite my inferno?
            I crossed over the Arno,
stone arch of the bridge just at daybreak,
            below the clock tower,
grieving, and there were three white birds on the water.

The first step into hell
            is to demonize,
to create an *other* : Berlusconi
            calls his detractors Commies,
and Bush says his support terror
            as he shreds our Constitution,
a pox on Madison's endeavors,
            the rich serving the rich
no less than in feudal manors,
            the American Medici
lining the pockets of the shamefully rich
            with Arab blood and Arab oil,
and where are his splendors,
            our Texas Medici, where
his hallmarks of civilization—

ash and rubble and a smirk;
cluster bombs, smart bombs . . .

with a bang and then a whimper, Possum.

Alessandro says the children
are rapidly forgetting
how all this has happened before.
Hence a school program
"to keep the memory alive."
Dove sta la memoria?

Lest one's former friends forget—
ah, Catullo! the worst indeed is the one
who once was an ally,
who once was our partisan.
Dante had a place for those who defiled the word.
I've seen Ugolino's cell, worn old hall
in the corner of the piazza
across from the elegance of the Medicis'.
Dante, under sentence of death,
composed his hell, he made his Paradiso.
He damned and praised.

In Coltano, I remembered,
        and in Venice,
and on the radio in Firenze—
        American poet on Italian radio again,
sixty years later,
        to speak *against* the fascists—
if poetry is a poet's religion,
        what happens to the practice
when a sacred trust is broken?
        Kannon, Kannon,

a President telling lies that lead to slaughter,
reporters repeating lies that lead to slaughter,
and what's a little feces in your burger
if it don't impede production
and thereby assures a profit?

        contra naturam

A moth escapes through a smoke hole
and nations crumble. A President lies
and a nation lies in rubble. When
one's allies can't be trusted,
the arts of even poetry will suffer,
and when there is no harmony in the heart,

when there is no loyalty to the word in one's heart,
there can be no allegiance.
No humanitas.

With usura
we have entered another age of savagery,
antiquities of Baghdad plundered,
wonders of the world sold for profit,
no house of good stone,
no manufactured Paradise of word or wood,
no temple made of words,
no real conviction, no sacrifice for the common good,
nor character in the man,
nor integrity in the work,
nor in the poem,

no Hikmet to rise from the bilge
and look up at the faces of his oppressors
        with a song in his heart
and courage enough to sing . . .
no don Pablo Neruda,
no real conviction.

Art ain't a bean-counter's business.
Though the beans need counting.

What is made to endure,
        what is made to live with,
cannot be commodified,
        is one with nature.
Is nature. Is our nature
        healing the heart with a song.
To be makers, not destroyers.

In Coltano, where the poet was caged,
        I remember.
And found, finally, just south of the road,

        beyond the narrow stand of pines,
a simple flag, a small hand-tied cross
        in a little square of junipers,
an indentation in the ground
        where a stone had stood
till the mayor of Pisa took it down
        to quell the bickering
of the Reds and the Blacks,
        but bickering is eternal—

now just a sheet of paper, a few sad facts
        protected from the drizzle
by plastic, where the Fascists held
        35,000, a small city,
Alessandro said, now long empty fields
        of silence, furrows cut straight
where Ezra sat, held by the Allies,
        reading the clouds,
searching the horizon
        for the white baptismal dome,
for the alabaster tip of the tower,
        caged panther
with his *Four Books* of Confucius,
        not yet assaying
the pain and wreckage of his hubris.

Ol' Ez, the Idyho Kid,
        lost among the Medicis.
And even despite his errors, his wreckage,
        there is great beauty
and not a little wisdom.

Just weeks before, Camilla drove us out
        to Rivalta,
the great medieval mansion
        miles across broad fields,
Piacenza,
        storehouse hung with thick hams

and strong cheeses,
    wine cellar stacked to the ceiling,

and across a dinner to die for
    looked at me with piercing eyes
and cried, "Too many mistakes!"
    "We make mistakes!"
Gray and I praised her,
    and our friend Sara praised her,
and Camilla cried, "Too many mistakes!"

Sweet Camilla, an Ezra,
    so beautiful, so determined
to orchestrate perfection: the struggle
    to organize the lit-fest, to find
the rose in the steel dust,
    flower of the eternal
in the transitory heart of the traveler.
    The flower that is
the lesson of the Buddha.

Oh, Italia, what people, what kindness
    in the hearts of people—
the mayor of San Giuliano
    brought me to talk with the council
and gave me the rainbow banner:
    Pace, a token.
Arturo brings me my poems from Bolzano,
    freshly into Italian,
and poems too from Alessandro.
    And when I speak against the war,
there are tears in Sara's eyes
    as she translates
into the French: Vaison la romaine,
    Provence,
birthplace of western Romantics—
    first time, she says,

she's ever wept in public.
        And tears again, listening
in Livorno.

Aieee! Thales cries,
        they have hope
who have nothing else.
        Where there is Kannon,
there is Kali, the destroyer.
        To believe in poetry
is to believe the heart can be opened,
        and in the commerce of the heart,
thrift is ruin.

Le Paradis n'est pas artificiel

Olga has embodied it in her song,
        and old Billyum,
translating Neruda, almost anonymous
        in the snows of Spokane.
The translator's art is provisional
        conclusion, the art
of the invisible. And I too
        have found life among the dead.
It's all there—not in the gift
        but in the giving,
living up to those few chosen words
        we can stand by
and die by when that time comes—
        just a few words,

(because it *is* so very difficult
        getting news from poetry,
news that stays news)

libertá, justice and mercy,
        a little love to thaw the heart in dead winter,
a little conviction we can live by.

Hayden embodies it,
     and sweet William—
what is made to endure, to live with.

I have tried to build a Paradise,
     a temple for poetry.
Now it threatens to crumble.
     Is this my hubris? Paradise
revealed by the eye of its maker?
     I am not
the megalomaniac Ezra,
     though I love him,
grieving for his errors,
     but am an American
where his cage once was,
where the old man called upon his gods.
I have my own errors to live with.

"When studying the work of the Masters,
I watch the working of their minds."

Here the long furrows for planting,
     deep rows of pine lining the roadway
to and from Coltano,
     gray doves silent,
farm dogs and manor dogs still barking,
     and out behind the store, a small club
where Partisans still dance on the weekends,
     the good smell of wood smoke,
everything passing.

Palms together: *gasshō.*
Kannon, Kannon, tomorrow
     the long road home,
long road stretching out behind:
the journey itself is home.

I lie awake in my narrow bed,
    sweating, on the banks of the Lethe,
listening to the voices of my dead:
    "These running dogs
of the Capitalist bourgeoisie,"
    KR intoned, and, "I write poetry
to seduce women . . . and to overthrow
    the Capitalist system—
in that order," and his grand guffaw.
    And Old Tom,
devoted to a lost revolution,
    "Time comes,
I got my gun." And he did.
    And he killed a man.
And it tormented all his days. Who could sing
    like no one sang in his
great Irish joy and Irish sorrow.
    And dear Denise
who found compassion
    even in "those groans men make,"
her simple cotton dresses and her tea,
    like steel in her conviction.
And the wars came and the wars changed.
    Another Third World country.
We stood for something—
    the word writ large:
to be makers, not destroyers.

Un poeta contro Bush
Un poeta contro la guerra

I have made a gift, whatever it's worth.
I stand for something.

The line between being murderers
and the accomplices of murderers
    and true resistance

does actually exist—cf.
     Albert Camus—
and me in a Marine Corps pup tent,
     Okinawa, forty years ago—
and a line between
     duplicity and truth.
By a few clear words and long practice,
     the vision.

A few words can change a life,
     which is a world.
I gather my masters
     in my hour of desolation.
The answer is in the poetry.
     The poetry
is my answer.
     Rumi after
September 11;
     Hikmet in the face of oppression;

and Hayden and Merwin,
     Adrienne, et alia
for almost anything—
     but always the mystery—
kadō—the way of poetry.

Kannon, Kannon,

the poem is a mystery, no matter
     how well crafted:
is a made thing
     that embodies nature.
And like Zen,
     the more we discuss it,
the further away . . .

Well, at least I *have* a few masters.
I have my practice.

Hayden says since his ex
       spiffed up
the little barn where he wrote through all those years,
       "It don't smell like cow piss
when it rains any more." Who knows something
       about Troubadours and the way of poetry,
about a Paradise made of words, knows
       there is no Paradise,
but there is Hell also within it—

(PART 2)
Akhmatova, at the prison gates,
       dares to testify of betrayal—
Hikmet, rising from the bilge,
       looks his oppressors in the face
              and sings—
Tu Fu survives long exile
       sustained by truth and conviction,
writing the poem.

My prison students often said,
"No good deed goes unpunished."

And Dante had a place
       for betrayers of trust—
those who betray their benefactors—
       ninth circle,
              ice for a Brutus, for a Cassius,
a temple of ice for a Judas.

I address you,
       Mr. Organizational Man,
as Rexroth addressed you
       in his elegy for Dylan Thomas
which you of course have not read:
       no fire in the belly,
nor fine old flame, no live tradition,
       no knowledge of the poem's worth,

nor of its making . . .
　　　no poetry in the life.

Were you among those
who walked Garcia-Lorca into the olive grove?

Quamdiu stat Copper Canyon,
stat et poesia Americanus;
Quando cadet Copper Canyon, cadet et poesia;
Quando cadet poesia, cadet et mundus.

Poetry is *not* a commodity,
　　　Mr. Literary Consultant
counting beans as they counted
　　　and sold the stones,
the wonder that was Rome—stone by stone
　　　measured in profit.

You think you can write an equation?

Poi che nel viso a certi li occhi porsi,
ne' quali 'l doloroso foco casca,
non ne conobbi alcun—
Dante, seventh circle,
recognizing no one—
eternal stranger, user or usurer alike—
sanza la qual chi sua vita consuma,
cotal vestigio in terra di sé lascia,
qual fummo in aere e in acqua la schiuma.

I am a man of no fortune.
You are one on whom the sun has gone down.

Perhaps your friends will explain it,
　　　if they can:
I mean the anger and passion of Su Tung-p'o,
　　　the invective

of dear old Catullo, betrayed
        by lover and by friend,
and exactly where in Dante's Hell
        one may discover
the temple of ice.

Would you author
the end of poetry's temple?
Collect your lucre
and get the hell out of town.

And also freshly departed
        from this temple
modeled on the practice of masters,
        Mr. born to privilege,
who'd belittle years of service,
        send a poet into exile
or forced retirement,
        a minor Tu Fu
who threatens the petty autocrat
        who's building a tin pot republic.

In the name of what gods or Muses,
this poison?

There is a Tao, a way to be followed.
        My fellow poets sustain it.
I have shored up my walls
        and manned my barricades
with those who embrace the tradition.

Forty years a monk, a life of service
        in a temple made of words—
and now it comes to this?

No good deed goes unpunished.

Stay and listen.
Resist the cry of Circe,
     for a moment,
         if you can—
ac ego in harum
ac vidi cadaveres animae—

and consider the word and the way:

A president telling lies,
     a bureaucrat telling lies,
         the press repeating lies . . .
a sacred trust dismissed, one's
     friends conspiring . . .
little deceits that are a kind of death . . .

to advance what agenda?

At what cost?
     And what then
is the value of the word?
     The word one stands by. And what
the foundation of our practice?

Say *government,* say *liberty,*
     say *poem.*
Each begins and ends
with the government of words.

     Shuo jen:

empty words from vacant hearts.
     And then what word, exactly,
shall we stand by? *Sinceritas:* standing
     beside one's word,
the Chinese written character
     portraying more than words can say,

the human figure, mouth open,
        precise definition—
the poet's commitment—
        the very life of poetry
depends on it, demands it—

poetry—that temple of words attended by
        its various monks and masters,
keepers and makers of its traditions.

        Saboteurs
in the temple of poetry,
        in the service of themselves only:
"The arrogance of bureaucrats stops at nothing,"
        Su Tung-p'o snarled—
betrayers, destroyers in the house of the maker:
        ninth circle for those
who betray a benefactor,
        an icy page in the book of the damned.

This is the house that poetry built:
        Copper Canyon first
and foremost
        through decades of struggle
                to find, to define
and clarify the vision . . .
        to sustain the practice attained
only through apprenticeship to masters.

This is the house that poetry built:
        deal with it, *mes frères,* or move on:
the art and history of the printed book,
        the art of the poem,
                the history of writing,
of poetry itself,
        several languages to fail at . . .
where every failure may be elevated into art . . .
        "Hardly the work of a mid-level bureaucrat,"

Su Tung-p'o observed. "Struggling to achieve
        simplicity, clarity itself,
is the life of the poem."

Charity is the answer,
the vision from long practice.
"I am a poet. I am
        a poet. I
am a poet."
        Ah, sweet Billyum the Elder,
you for whom it took so very long to say it,
        what would you say to those
who discredit the struggle?
I have a tradition, ancestry;
and when I damn you,
you shall stay well-damned
in a fine old tradition.

Kannon, Kannon,
to forgive is one thing,
to forget, another.

Words have ancestry and progeny,
        our lives made of words,
our character shaped by words.
        Actions have consequence, *mes frères:*
see how the moth escapes through the smoke hole,
        how the sun
burns through the clouds above Taishan
        and the whole heavens open,
blue and yet transparent,
        just as the old painters portrayed it,
                this Tuscan light,
how "the ant's a centaur in his dragon world,"
        music sustaining the vision of affection
                for this suffering world—

What matters, Ez sez,
        is the quality of the affection—
how the poem
        embodies the vision in its rhythm,
the rhythm the test, Ez sez,
        of the poet's *sinceritas*,
energy of discovery or revelation—

"what thou lovest well remains . . . "

What arises from long tradition
        sustains us,
refreshing water
        from the ancient well,
the quality of Socrates' affection.

Kannon, Kannon,
all praise possible
only by contrast with damnation—
beauty born in ugliness,
a Paradise in the bowels of Hell.

And it happens in ordinary words,
        ordinary words
that lead lives into transformation
        every day, or can lead
lives into Hell, and do, every day,
        by those who dishonor the word:
Americans burned
        and hung on display
                in Fallujah,
a modern crucifixion, and what
        brought them to that destiny
but empty words from dishonest men,
        words from Baudelaire's *hypocrite lecteur!*
Captured Iraqis humiliated,
        photographed naked,

in degrading sexual positions,
  or in women's underwear,
American GIs laughing, attaching
  electrodes to their genitals,
torture as American as
  that proverbial pie.
    Why lie?

Every war produces savages
from amongst the almost civilized.
There's always an Abu Ghraib, a My Lai.
Death is the triumph of bureaucracy.
Cadaveres animae.

Hypocrite lecteur!
A little poetry might've saved them,
a little honest self-reflection.

The Torah, woven from
  the Ineffable Name,
is a living body of words;
  the ineffable,
the unnamable, the Word of God
  and the Devil's Dictionary,
all ordinary words;
  the Book of Ruth,
Mein Kampf, the Song of Songs
  Tao Te Ching and the Bodhisattva Vow,
all ordinary words, poetry
  understood only as deeply
as one finds courage to live it.

Shiva the Maintainer,
Shiva the Destroyer.

Now the children of Abraham and the children of Muhammad
  unite

in mutual ritual slaughter:
        Sharon with his word for justice,
Arafat with his word for justice,
        al Qaeda and the Taliban
with their own gates to Heaven,
        and every son-of-a-Bush
with golden keys
        to a private ivory Paradise—

eternal slaughter,
        contra naturam,
killing for empty words
        and vacant promises
and a profit by those who engineer it.

All you need do is keep faith
with a few well-chosen words
and you shall find your Paradise
or the Hell of your betrayal.

When the head bean-counter's fit
        to argue the relative merits
of the morning glory in Chiyo-ni's bucket,
        I'm inclined to trust him.
Character is not about the beans,
        but about commitments.

The real subject of poetry, Tu Fu cries,
        is character,
character built and defined
        by ordinary words we stand by,
made exemplary by a poet's craft and vision,
        each deed by proper word defined,
who can draw from the air
        a live tradition,
and from many a fine old eye
        that same unconquerable flame—

Ezra knew it
    in his cage,
        old panther not yet broken,
the very life of poetry, the poet's timeless vision:

Though his beauty lies in shards,
    in fragments among his ruins,
there is a glimpse of Paradise within it . . .
    and of the Hell to come,
the Hell of his own making.

Vanity brought him down,
    error in the diffidence that faltered,
        caged panther
with his poem "including history,"
    his wreckage all about him,
shards and fragments of great beauty.

Go ask Hayden what it means
    to sabotage his editor;
go ask Merwin, Dave Lee,
    or my own dearest Olga;
ask Shirley Kaufman what it means to live
    in a war-torn city
        whose answer to death is death,
and struggle to keep faith in poetry.
    Ask whether I'm an answer
or a problem.

Mr. Expert is dead wrong.

If the reader were the publisher's master,
    he might as well sell pornography
and reach the broader spectrum . . .
    but the poem, the book,
is text, edifying and enlightening,
    illuminating, bearing

unsettling witness . . . ah,
        unsettling: its function
as much didactic
        as entertaining.

Praise the blossoming cherry,
        each bud cherished the more
                for its transience,
as Saigyō said a thousand years ago.

What values are eternal?

They tell me, "Poetry is dead."

Would you kiss a D'Annunzio,
        that Fascist fop,
before the bruised lips of Odysseus?
        "Hast'ou found a nest
softer than cunnus?" Sweet Ez.
        K'ung-fu Tzu says,
"One who doesn't blink
        when nose-to-nose with the tiger
is fit to lead."

I could show you a poor man's Paradise,
        already there within you,
but you would say,
        "It isn't real."
See how you already turn away.
        Not from poetry
comes your version of wisdom,
        not from poetry your perfidy.

"Europe wants something more solid
        and more real than poetry."
—Leopardi, June, 1826,
        about the time Hugh Glass explored

the headwaters of the Missouri;
        and Wordsworth and our brother Percy
vivified western nature verse
        thanks in part to Arabic precedents,
craft and concept filtered through Provence;
        Japan was closed to the world,
thirty years before Perry's cannons blew open the gates,
        but the poetry of wilderness and garden
blossomed everywhere, Bashō their master,
        Ryōkan at the height of his power
when Issa died that year.

In English-American, our verse went soft,
        sentimental flowers
                appealing to the masters of the parlor,
soft in the belly, but for Whitman
        and a handful of others,
Dickinson among them,
        who invented American verse,
or laid at least the cornerstones for Ezra,
        eighty years later, Ez
                demanding a poetry
more solid, more real—
        "harder, saner,
                hewn closer to the bone."
"At least as well-written as prose."

The White House believed it could co-opt
Whitman, Dickinson and Hughes?
Tell'em the poets thought not.
Nothing's more solid than the poem.

Now somewhere in the southern Tyrol,
        Arturo Zilli struggles to buy time
to find a way to bring the poetry—
        word and essence beyond word—
from one tongue to another;

and a few hundred miles southward,
Alessandro leaves his child
        to return to the solitude
of books and papers, long hours alone
        that bind us as brothers;
and ten thousand miles east,
        our Brother Yusuke
in his own humble temple,
        fashioned from the words of his masters,
dips his brush
and bends over that same poem.

There is a Paradise in service
        to one's Muses,
                an order in the temple.
I bend over Lao Tzu's ancient text:
        "Beauty and ugliness
have one origin," and every war,
        two losers.
An elegance in bowing to one's masters.
And: "Taking the place of a great artisan,
        rare is the one who escapes
without self-inflicted wounds."

Pull down thy vanity.
Learn of the green world . . .
Poetry is my answer.

Winter snows fall on the Alps,
        on Pisa, on Taishan
                and on Sanjo-shi.
Then spring cherry-blossom-time again.
        There is a heart, a history,
                behind every poem.
Merwin claims, rightly, I believe,
        it's the unknown,
                the unknowable

working its secret magic
        and no exact equation
can make it happen.

Translation is one key
        to unlock the mystery,
providing perspective and tradition.
        "Make it new! Make it new!"
Make it new somehow
        within a defined tradition.
Lu Chi holds an answer,
        "When studying the masters . . . "

And yet the mystery remains:
        to be in the service of words,
of words in their richest music,
        music lifting anima and mind
to reveal another secret,
        always another secret,
within another secret.

There's no equation for the poem.

If the poet's work weren't secret
        even to the poet,
                anyone could do it,
and it's a fool thinks anyone can.

One's karma is earned as the dharma is practiced.

You want to surpass a poet
        in this temple of poesy?
We'll lock minds like the old Chinese.
        The poem unlocks the life,
opens the heart, defines
        and assays the practice.
It is the koan, the book of the dead,

the apocalypse, the book
of revelation. The poem,
        only the poem.

What's at stake is merely everything.
Can't you see it?

Kannon, Kannon,

the lies of our president, deceits
        of those who called themselves
our allies in the word,
        as they betrayed the word . . .
how shall I address them?

I have provided a model.
I built an altar.
But I can't make one choose it.
I know what I have given.
Error in the diffidence that faltered.

Deceit is a Hell of its own.
        And now it is yours, *mon freres,*
who own it.
        It *is* so very difficult
                getting news from poetry,
news that stays news,
        so listen closely:
I return like Odysseus,
        from three years wandering a wilderness,
three years of great darkness,
        to plant my oar in my homeland sand.
Poetry is my true Penelope,
        my wife and my mistress.
I call upon my masters
        in my hour of desolation.
I have made a Paradise . . .
        of sorts.

I have it within me.
Poetry sustains it.
Fire and ice await the destroyers,
but for the makers, a kind of Paradise.

But you must write in your own blood
      what word you stand by
           to attain it,
you must write it out in blood:
      only by patience and perseverance,
         the vision;
only by the courage of practice
      may one attain it.

Even from the icy bowels of the ninth circle,
      there is a way out,
         a light,
and where there's light, a source—
      we've only to follow the light,
         returning—
oh, the thought of what America might be like
      if poetry had a wide circulation—
returning to the source
      provides an answer,
a glimpse of the way to Paradise.

Paradise, Elytis says,
      is made of the same exact material
as Hell, and both dwell within,
      and the two make one,
crystallized, revealed within the poem.

First just a pale light,
      faint, over the marshlands,
         daybreak,
faint pale light
      beyond the soft gray fog of unknowing,

and then the breath,
        heartbeat of the poem, rising
into its dear dance with Eros
        and its dance with death,
                its own inevitable calling . . .
touch of consonant and vowel,
        not a Circe calling men to her sty,
but the Muse who refuses The Lie . . .

Is it sun or moon
        shines just now
through our heartache?
        Shines through foibles and slanders,
and ultimately binds.
        I have made a gift.
I know what I have made.

What thou lovest well remains.

Old poet, freed from his cage,
        spent thirteen years in the loony-bin,
translating Confucius: "One's Paradise
        is one's own good nature."
All wisdom in calling things
        by their right names.
It was the uncommonly good, sound
        practical advice of his own
that he forgot to follow.

The great poem has room for failures
        among its successes,
and the panther had many, his snarl
        worse, mostly, than his bite,
megalomania not least among them,
        and the arrogance of that god-awful
stupid suburban prejudice . . .
        nevertheless,

            a quality of light
in his telling the tale of his tribe.

Qualities of light in the passion, rage and sass,
        great love of learning
                in a pompous ass . . .
who believed in the poem as few ever have,
        old poet in the cage,
                old savage, savvy messiah.
It's true, all true,
        whatever you say of him is true.
And yet the poem endures
        in all its complexity,
                its moments

of uncompromising beauty.
It the temple of words,
the poem is master.
The poem. Only
the poem.

It is a path to enlightenment.

It's yours if you've courage and will
        to grasp it, to "grasp the azure"
of Master K'ung or Ol' Ez at his best,
        as in the very bowels of Hell
there is also a Paradise
        attainable,
made of the same mind and heart,
        but you must open your eyes
to see those clouds begin to part above Taishan,
        how the whole sky begins to open,
                transparent blue,
silence broken
        only by breath and heartbeat,
open eyes and heart to the poem—

to the heart from the ear,
to the mind from the eye—

the epiphany of the poem,

wherein all is music,
all is light.

After a Winter of Grieving

Before I traveled my road I was my road.
        —Antonio Porchia

No road leads the way.
The road follows behind.
        —Takamura Kotarō

With the moon so bright,
I could not sleep, the garden
glowing in cold white light.

I rose, dressed, and went out
to the deck to sit in the cold and think.

The April moon was full and high,
almost big enough to burst,
haloed by a ring of sparkling light
and a few bright stars.

The garden Buddha, a pretty boy,
wore an apron of moss.

The old Moon Watching Pavilion,
where I watched this moon with my daughter

nearly thirty years ago,
rots under the katsura tree.

I watched the first gray light begin to seep
through the trees before
the first robin arrived. Each gain,
each loss, had a name I could not speak.

Denise called this, "A kind
of Paradise," this logged-off scrappy land
I came to thirty years ago,
impoverished by my needs.

Paradise is a sometime thing,
wherever one might make it—
a river of stones, bamboo, a foreign tree,
building a home alone—

and this same old moon,
eternally new
in geologic time.

The road to Kage-an is gone.
Don't ask me where I've been.
The road out is the road in.

Notes on Traveling Companions

SAPPHO (CA. 630 B.C.E.)
Born on Lesbos, Sappho was exiled for political reasons sometime between 604 and 596, and returned in 581, when a general amnesty was granted to all political prisoners and exiles. She is credited with inventing the Mixo-Lydian mode, a diatonic scale corresponding to our G minor, that later became known as the Gregorian Mode, the foundation of the "heavenly music" of the early Catholic Church. She may be called the mother of western feminism. In a fit of depression, she committed suicide by diving from the cliffs of Lesbos and drowning in the sea.

ANAKREON (CA. 570 B.C.E.)
Just younger than Sappho, Anakreon was a lyric poet from Teos who wrote elegiac and iambic drinking poems in the Ionic dialect. His life was devoted to the love of women and boys, and to song. He claimed to be in love with his Muse, Bacchus, and Eros. He is said to have lived to the age of 85.

ASKLEPIADOS (CA. 320 B.C.E.)
Asklepiados was a grammarian from Myrleia about whom little is known. A handful of his lyrics and fragments survive in the *Greek Anthology*.

CATULLUS (CA. 60 B.C.E.)
Gaius Valerius Catullus was born in Verona, ca. 84 B.C.E., to a socially elite family who dined with Julius Caesar. But the poet's remarks on sycophancy became famous as he devoted himself entirely to poetry, forming the *Poetae Novi* with his friend Calvus (Gaius Licinius Macer) and a group of poets. They wrote in colloquial Latin filled with literary

allusion, personal observation, and metrical mastery, and some lifted from the classical Greek of Sappho and Callimachus. Catullus is presumed to have died by the age of thirty.

Lao Tzu (ca. 500 b.c.e.)

Lao Tzu, meaning the "Old Master," was a contemporary of Confucius. His true name, according to the *Records of the Historian*, was Li Erh Tan and he was an archivist of the Chou court in Lo-yang. Confucius remarked after meeting Lao Tzu, "I have been face-to-face with a dragon."

Chuang Tzu (369–286 b.c.e.)

The *Chuang Tzu* is one of the most beloved books in all of history. Master Chuang's nonconformity, and his use of parallelism, antithesis, paradox and humor, make him a unique sage in the worlds of Taoism and Zen. Little is known of his origins or of his life, but his importance to Eastern thought is as vast as that of Plato in the West. Bashō wouldn't leave home without him. Translated with J. P. Seaton.

Lu Chi (261–300)

Born on the Yangtze Delta in 261, Lu Chi was a strapping young man, over six feet, from a prosperous family noted for producing military leaders. He was obsessed with learning, and, following a military defeat, he and his younger brother fled into exile, where they "barred the door for ten years and studied the classics." His *Wen Fu* (*The Art of Writing*) has been a source of wisdom and inspiration for countless generations of Asian masters.

Wang Wei (701–761)

Imprisoned at the Bodhi Temple in the capital city of Ch'ang-an during the An Lu-shan Rebellion, Wang Wei emerged as one of China's first great Buddhist poets. He was also greatly admired as a landscape painter and musician. His poetry as is crisp and uncluttered as a Zen garden.

Li Po (701–762)

Imprisoned as a traitor, pardoned, exiled, celebrated, granted amnesty, Li Po lived on the edge and spent his life turning himself into an almost mythic being. He was a consummate panhandler and an epic drinker who claimed he never revised a poem. He probably wrote more kinds of poetry in more styles than any other classical Chinese poet. Legend says he drowned in the Yellow River, drunk, trying to embrace the reflection of the moon.

TU FU (712–770)

The "Poetry Sage" was born to a family that had once been part of nobility, but whose fortune had declined. He spent years in poverty, wandering, studying, a model of Confucian rectitude as he protested war and conscription and unfair taxation. His poetry went unacknowledged during his lifetime and about five-sixths of it was lost forever, only 1554 poems surviving from among the 10,000 he wrote. Kenneth Rexroth called him "the greatest non-epic, non-dramatic poet in all of history."

YUAN CHEN (779–831)

A controversial poet, Yuan Chen suffered banishment and exile for giving voice to his social conscience. His elegies are among the most profoundly moving personal poems of the T'ang dynasty, and an autobiographical piece became the story line for the Yuan dynasty drama, *The Dream of the Red Chamber*.

SU TUNG-P'O (1036–1101)

Also known as Su Shih, Su Tung-p'o was deeply schooled in *Chuang Tzu* and *Tao Te Ching* before devoting himself to Zen Buddhism. Caught up in the political intrigues of his time, he suffered banishments, but proved to be a compassionate and benevolent administrator in the provinces while writing some of the greatest poetry of the Sung dynasty.

LI CH'ING-CHAO (1084–1151)

When her husband died young, the consequences for Li Ch'ing-chao were both emotionally and socially devastating. She had been raised as a "liberated woman," taught to read and write and to love scholarship, and with her husband had compiled an immense catalogue of stone and bronze vessels. When her second husband proved to be abusive, she summoned the rare (in her age) courage to leave him. She is generally considered to be classical China's greatest female poet.

SAIGYŌ (1118–1190)
Born to a famous military family in the Fujiwara clan, Saigyō took Buddhist vows when he was twenty-three, and became Japan's most influential poet in the long rich tradition of Buddhist nature poetry. He was a model and inspiration for Bashō, Issa, Ryōkan, and many other poets.

IKKYŪ (1394–1481)
When Ikkyū was appointed head of Japan's largest temple complex at Daitokuji in Kyoto, he lasted nine days before denouncing the monks for hypocrisy and inviting them to argue their differences "in the sake parlors and whorehouses" with him. He later returned to Daitokuji after fires had decimated the compound and oversaw rebuilding. He revolutionized shakuhachi (bamboo flute) music, helped bring Zen to Noh drama, refined the tea ceremony, and was a renowned calligrapher. At seventy, he fell in love with a blind singer and scandalized the Buddhist community by moving her into his quarters in the temple and writing erotic poems about their love affair.

BASHŌ (1644–1694)
Born Matsuo Munefusa to a samurai family, Bashō single-handedly elevated haiku and haibun (poetry/prose in combination) to high literary arts. His travelogues are non pareil. Many a Japanese poet has told me, "Haiku began and ended with Bashō."

BUSON (1715–1783)
A devoted family man and a highly successful painter, Buson's haiku often reflects a painter's eye and a rich complexity. He did not share Bashō's classicism, nor his Zen discipline, but composed consciously, developing a poetics of enhanced sensibility and evocation.

RYŌKAN (1758–1831)
Ryōkan was a Soto Zen monk who lived by his begging bowl, wandering the mountainous "snow country" of Niigata province. He took a

Zen name, "Daigu," or "Great Fool," and wrote Chinese style poems as well as haiku and tanka, and in his old age fell in love with a young nun, with whom he exchanged remarkable love poems. His last days were spent as a groundskeeper at a Shinto shrine.

Issa (1763–1827)
Issa took a solemn vow at age 29 to follow "the Way of Poetry." His masterwork, *The Spring of My Life*, modeled on Bashō's haibun travelogues, reveals a lifetime of tragedy, hardship, humor and love. Sometimes a little sentimental, often ironic, his poetry was earned. He once looked squarely into the eyes of a very dangerous daimyo and told him he would not reduce his art to the level of local dilettantes. He was a gentle eccentric who loved and was loved by children especially.

Yosano Akiko (1878–1942)
Yosano Akiko wrote more than 75 books, including twenty volumes of poetry and the definitive translation into modern Japanese of *The Tale of Genji*. She was Japan's first modern feminist, and championed the causes of pacifism and social reform. When she publicly criticized the emperor over the Russo-Japanese War of 1904, her house was stoned for three long years. She gave birth to a dozen children whom she supported alone through literary endeavors, often enduring severe poverty. Her erotic tanka, first published at the turn of the century, created a scandal. Today that literary period is called The Age of Akiko. Translated with Keiko Matsui Gibson.

Jaan Kaplinski (b. 1941)
Born in Tartu, Estonia, Kaplinski was raised by his mother after his father disappeared into Stalin's labor camps. He studied Romance languages and linguistics at Tartu State University and has translated Polish and Chinese as well as Romance languages. Today he is one of Europe's leading poets. Translated with the poet and Riina Tamm.

Sam Hamill was born in 1943 and orphaned during World War II. Following a tour of duty in the U. S. Marine Corps (1961–65), he attended L. A. Valley College and the University of California, Santa Barbara, where he was an award-winning editor. He is the Founding Editor of Copper Canyon Press and was Editor from 1972 to 2004. He taught in prisons for fifteen years and has worked extensively with battered women and children; he has been a magazine and newspaper columnist, literary and book arts critic, letterpress printer, and has edited definitive editions of the poetry of Thomas McGrath and Kenneth Rexroth. For nine years, he directed the Port Townsend Writers Conference, and in January 2003, he founded Poets Against the War. He has published fourteen volumes of original poetry, three volumes of literary essays, and more than two-dozen books translated from classical Chinese, Japanese, Greek, Latin, and Estonian. He has been the recipient of awards from the National Endowment for the Arts, the Guggenheim Foundation, the Lila Wallace–Readers Digest Fund, the Andrew Mellon Fund, the U.S.-Japan Friendship Commission, and has received two Washington State Governor's Awards. His work has been translated into Japanese, Chinese, Greek, Italian, Dutch, Portuguese, Croatian, and Lithuanian.